Where is Love?

Copyright 2013 by Prose

All rights reserved. No part or portion of this book
may be reproduced or stored in any form without
author's consent.

For permission contact:

Write in Black, Inc.

www.writeinblackinc.com

(862) 200-PENS

Typesetting & editing: Write in Black, Inc.

Cover by: Draw in Black, Inc., New Jersey

ISBN: 978-0-9891279-0-5

Library of Congress Cat. Num. in Publication Data

Printed in the United States of America

To my previous lovers

my friends

my family
&
my ancestors

Oh... I almost forgot the haters
Love you guys the most.
Thanks for the inspiration!

Where Is Love?

Disclaimer: The ideas and conclusions expressed in this work are mine alone and as such; one or more conclusions may not meet your approval. However, the purpose of this book is to open a dialogue and examine what may possibly be one of the most common human problems of all. Something is very wrong in the way that we love each other and it is my desire that my work will arouse in you a holistic understanding of our ties to those we love, an understanding of what spawned the ties and how to protect & strengthen those bonds. I wish you much success and hope that I have done a great service to all that read this book.

This book, although based on true-life experiences, has been fictionalized and does not depict any actual person. Resemblance to any real people living or dead is absolutely coincidental. By virtue of the reader seeing this statement and continuing to read each ensuing page thereafter, you have provided your approval and have forfeited any right to petition this work.

Table of Contents

TABLE OF CONTENTS   V

FOREWORD   VII

DEDICATION   XIII

PREFACE   XVI

CHAPTER 1 - RELATIONSHIP REFLECTION: HOW IT STARTS...   1

TO PICK OR NOT BE PICKED....   1

OK, SO WHAT ABOUT SOME RESEARCH? WE DO IT FOR EVERYTHING ELSE...   5

USING X-RAY VISION... ON TAKING A LOOK INSIDE...   8

LADIES... PLEASE PAY ATTENTION BECAUSE THIS IS THE ANSWER TO YOUR MILLION DOLLAR QUESTION ON MEN AND OUR MESSED UP THOUGHT PROCESS...   14

7-8 MINUTES OF CONVO IS ALL IT TAKES... THE GOLDEN MOMENT...   27

MEN COME FROM THE DUNGEON AND WOMEN COME FROM SOMEWHERE ELSE...   31

DESTROYING THE MYTH OF THE GOLD-DIGGER...   33

CHAPTER 2 – BREAKING DOWN BARRIERS   41

YOUNG BOYS & THEIR THINGS; OLD MEN & THEIR QUESTIONS (THEY TALK THAT WAY BECAUSE THAT'S THE BEST FORM OF COMMUNICATION THEY CAN MUSTER)...   41

SHARING YOUR EMOTIONAL STATE... THE RITE THAT BINDS!   56

Where Is Love? vi

MR. RIGHT HURTS WHEN SHE CAN'T ACCEPT HIM; BUT STOP BITCHING... WE DO IT TO THEM ALL THE TIME! 62

WOMEN FANTASIZE – EVERYBODY LIKES ME; MEN PONDER – DOES SHE LIKE ME... 74

YOU FUCKING BASTARDS... THE MARRIED AND WOMANIZING! 84

CHAPTER 3 – APPLYING WHAT U LEARNED 95

OK, NO MORE GAMES... KEEPING IT REAL, HOW ABOUT KEEPING IT HONEST? 95

LOVE DON'T HURT YOU (THE PROOF) 1 COR. 13:4-8 100

PICKING & TIMING... 110

OOOOOH, YOU SOOO NASTY... YEAH RIGHT. GROW UP! 116

IF YOU HAVEN'T GOTTEN IT YET... LET ME BE CLEAR [THE TECHNIQUES]... 141

FINAL THOUGHTS 154

FOREWORD

By Curt Haskins

Okay. Here I go... finally braving my fears and putting to print a book that I have been carrying around in my dayum head for at least the past 15 years. Honestly the prerequisite thoughts have been there my whole life, but in my adult years, I finally matured to the point where I could confront my personal intimacy issues and deal with the opposite sex in particular.

So who am I... nobody special: just a regular, everyday guy trying to find his extraordinary equal. I thought that by the time I wrote this darn thing, I would have become either financially successful from my earlier entrepreneurial endeavors or I would have found the love of my life.

Regardless, I have to be honest: There is the potential that maybe everything I am about to share is pure cacha, considering that this is a self-help book that didn't even help its author as of yet. Then again, I have always been able to help everyone else get what they needed while neglecting my very own needs.

Where Is Love?

Anyhow, seeing as how I am getting older, I can't just wait until everything is perfect, and if there is anything that life has taught me it's that when you have a thought to share, or a compliment to give, or a statement to make, just go ahead and do it! Shoot, what are you waiting for?

As you can see, I am a real person. I use profanity, hell, I outright love to; but in hopes of being able to elevate us all, I have chosen to refrain from hiding my intelligence, so that I might challenge the readers to think on a higher level. I believe that the overall content that I provide is laced with hidden jewels that will enrich the lives of all of you that are honest enough to embrace them and put them to use in the personal relationships of your daily lives.

Now you might say, what makes your book so different from every other book on love, and I would have to say that I have seen and read numerous books on love. There seems to be a pattern that exists in them, where problems are always pointed out and presented in a way that causes all the readers to feel connected.
Establishing this "me too" factor becomes the focus of these books.

FOREWORD   ix

By doing this, camaraderie is created, but no solutions
are given. The idea of solving the critical issues remains
unaddressed. This was my main concern; if I was gonna
say what's wrong... I was gonna be sure to tell you how
to fix it. Additionally, I wanted to give you the rationale
behind the issues that cause failure in relationships.
Too often we can recognize popular causes, but don't
understand them. This leaves room for them to reoccur.
This is the introductory volume in a set of three, aimed
at teaching all of my brothers and sisters to love. Since
it seemed easiest to start by speaking to you all in an
intimate way, I felt most comfortable addressing the
microcosmic view of love:

1] Eros, love between 2 people, namely intimacy
between a person and their mate

2] Philia, brotherly love, concern for the well being of
another as an intimate (friend or family)

3] Agape, love as a sacrifice for the uplift of another's
spiritual needs

Although we mostly concentrate on Eros, it is the
combination of all 3 types that is the genesis of love in
partnering human beings.

Where Is Love?   x

I want to say that my whole heart has been poured into this book because I felt the need to try to reach out to the world and fulfill my purpose by teaching us to love. I was a teacher in my past and I had the desire burning in me to help steer the present generation towards a state of realization where these unfairly emotionally robbed youth could gain a moment to exhale... a chance to not just catch their breath, but to also learn to think under pressure and develop solutions to the problems that face them. The world has been awakened to the needs of the youth nearly 3 generations ago, but in the last two, the ball has been dropped and now the phenomena of children raising children has ripped the very fabric of basic intimacy from the hearts and minds of the youth of society. They have no heroes! There isn't a voice crying out in this wilderness pointing them towards a path that will lead them to rescue.

I, like so many, tried to lay that groundwork from within a decrepit system that ignores this need in preference of "dumbing them down", so that they become little more than animals of labor.

FOREWORD

xi

But I took an oath, and since I couldn't stay true through the traditional means of standing in front of the class, I have chosen to speak publicly and then to place those thoughts and words in this book and give them clarity. Because this time, when knowledge gets put in the book... I am going to be sure to teach them to look there. From one normal person to another, thanks for picking up my book and I advise you to strap yourselves in... because this is going be one helluva ride!

Where Is Love?   xii

DEDICATION

I'd like to dedicate this book to the women who loved me so well during a time in my life when I couldn't reciprocate. That was a low point for me as a man... because it was the first time I realized that I was still a boy in a man's body *acting* grown. I now realize all the disappointment, hurt and scars I definitely caused and want to apologize for not being mature enough or better yet, courageous enough to address the deficit when it presented itself.

The words and thoughts expressed in this book greatly reflect the knowledge that I gained from those mistakes. At the time, I wanted to be cherished by you all, but deep down, I honestly never thought I deserved to be shown even the slightest attention and that made me work hard to sabotage anything that began to seem like it was going to go good for me. I thank you for showing me what it felt like to be loved, because I needed that.

Your sacrifices, brought back to mind a multitude of lost lessons on love that my Nanda had taught me to carry inside of my heart when I was a little boy.

Where Is Love? xiv

From our experiences and Nanda's teachings, I was able to exile myself to the inner sanctum of my soul and begin a healing process that led to my ultimate maturation and ultimately my celebration of becoming the man I always wanted to know, learn from and be. I can now share with others what I've learned in how to love and be loved.

From the bottom of my heart... I THANK YOU!

Without you, there would be no book.

Look Sheri...it's done! You said I had this in me.

I want to publicly tell you that you are always a part of my success, as you were the catalyst for me overcoming my procrastination.

Baby Sis... you are such a sweet woman, ideally I would want my wife to have a great many of your qualities.

Thanks for holding me down...

we all we got!

Ms. Dayle... Thank you for just pushing me to hurry. You have no idea how invaluable you made yourself to this process.

DEDICATION

Nikki G. I don't know where you are, but you were my first independent love. In fact your impact was so strong I had to write about you for a whole section of the book. Years have passed and I swear I have done my best to find you. I know every woman that is from my intimate circle may feel slighted by my reference to you but I know that I would give up anyone to be with you... it's just that simple and if I ever find you... I will make that happen!

Finally, I guess if I have to dedicate this book to someone special, it should be dedicated to L, my bestest buddy in the whole world, because she has been able to stay faithful to loving me as a friend, even with all of my issues and my consistent lack of contact.

I have made more unfulfilled promises to L than I have to anyone in this world... and yet she somehow still manages to love me. This is where I have learned a great deal about love from. If ever a woman came close to my idea of perfection it is you Lina Rieger.

I love you with all my heart and soul!
J... take care of our treasure... its your job now!

PREFACE

I believe that when you take a look at your past relationships you'll find a common denominator... the most prevalent problem in them... is selection. Selection sets the wheels in motion and initiates the pairing. It is the catalyst for engaging in the tying together of each partner's heart, so your selection needs to be grounded in some examination to ensure that your needs get met in the relationship. When engaging in building rapport between yourself and that special someone, there needs to be a process put forth by you on your behalf to make certain that this person is capable of meeting that need. Time must be spent, so that regret doesn't become a reoccurring theme.

There needs to be an understanding of the psyche of men/women regarding how they choose their mate and why. For men, he either wants to be engaged, or he wants to be nurtured, or if he's ready... he wants his complement.

For women, she may want to be connected to someone, she may be seeking security, she may be searching for the person that completes her or she may want a place to belong... a family of her own.

PREFACE   xvii

But alas... how do we interchange these concepts...
there is only one way... and that's by dialogue. We
must learn to talk to each other. We must become
accustomed to knowing when, how and what we can
disclose to one another. It's most advantageous to be
able to share it all, though everyone may not be strong
enough to do so at first. There must be an appreciation
for each partner's individuality and a support for that
individualism as well. Men must take the lead and not
continue to make excuses that allow us to seek
acceptance of our deficits as a true partner. Very often,
I do harp on the men more, because the present
epidemic of broken and saturated love is a direct failure
of us accepting our role as the leader of our families.
I'm not talking in terms of being some dictator in the
home, but as a spiritual force committed to the well-
being and success of those souls entrusted to your care.
Men, we need to own up to our role as the provider,
because ALL women are searching for security... period!
The men get back to their place of greatness when they
learn to communicate and learn whom their perspective
mate is... they create an interest in their mate by their
exploration.

Where Is Love?   xviii

By their leadership, men recreate the bonds of confidence. When men allow themselves to be vulnerable this becomes the rite that binds.

Even with all of this, there are certain biological differences in how we present ourselves in a relationship. How we love is experienced a certain way, based on certain criteria. It's critical to understand the damage of rejecting the good efforts of someone who has minimal experience loving. This can lead to the misogynistic acts that have become commonplace in our society.

The surfacing norms create a mentality in youth of both sexes where she thinks *everyone* likes her, and he wonders whether *anyone* likes him. What a vast difference in ascertaining security in their place in their relationships!

Ladies, how about loving yourselves and knowing your worth? This prevents men from acting without conscience... like all their blingy things matter most. How unfortunate, considering that she likes him more, when he simply gives himself rather than his things. Even worse is the fact that the ladies don't even expect much from the men.

PREFACE

It is now time to recognize each other fully and reestablish love among us all. There is no more room for the foolishness that has pushed us so far away from each other.

Where is love...

It's in us!

Has been all the time, but we have got to rediscover it by being honest, rather than opting for what fits our comfort zone. Love is beautiful and I have proof of what it should look like.

Love — it's the ability to recognize and implement a method of sharing your heart unconditionally with the person that inspires you to be your absolute best... so where the F is it at?

Where Is Love?

Chapter 1 - Relationship Reflection: How it Starts...

Throughout all the world I have sought a state of liberty. It wasn't until I decided to exercise my choices that I began to attain those things I most craved. – C Haskins

To Pick or not be Picked....

Ok, so I only recently came to accept the possibility of a lot of the ideas expressed in this book. This, in fact, is the latest of those thoughts. Everyone wants to be liked by everyone else and we feel special when we are selected. Take for example when we are youth playing basketball; the kids gather around and pick two captains. These captains then pick from the lot, the most talented and athletic players to the least skilled, most unwanted youth on the court. In this manner, the captain moves to ensure a win. So it's a match of wits between the selectors and a rally of roller-coaster highs and lows for the emotions of the candidates.

It's a mini victory just getting selected to play... it's the instant reward that every child needs to validate their self-worth.

Where Is Love?

This sort of mentality is learned back then, and stays with us well into our adult years, so it feels appropriate when we use that same methodology in the aspect of our lives that we most want to "win" in. I experienced the same flattering feeling whenever a woman decided that I was the one... that I felt when I was chosen to "ball up." I was being picked, so I must be valuable, valid... I matter to someone!

Hmmm... getting picked to me symbolized my value. So I basically was a trophy on display with all the accouterment that came along with that. I got put on display in front of everyone. I was kept shiny when company was around, but set aside, dusty and unengaged otherwise. I was an accomplishment, not a complement. What's worse is that I was perfectly fine with that. In fact, I preferred it that way, but why?

My flattery beyond measure for being chosen made me feel obligated to be the chooser's man. That really isn't logical... I mean referring to the logic I applied to a winning team selection, if *I* wanted to win, *I* would do the picking!

Chapter 1 - Relationship Reflection

If *I* want to get good grades and excel in school, then *I* put forth the effort and select topics that *I* can excel in. If *I* want a great friend, *I* choose the person *I* like and move towards establishing rapport.

Yet, when it came to the most significant of social interactions, *I* left it up to chance for *my* happiness to be determined. *I* let someone else choose what was supposed to make *me* happy. Hmmm... no research: just allow myself to be selected, not even knowing whether this person is a great person, or whether she has first-rate conversation skills, or a good sense of humor. So I guess I'm trying to win without choosing the best player... pretty stupid hungh? But why?

What I hadn't considered was that in a situation like this, I lose my control. Therefore, whatever deficit she has ... that's what *I* get. Her way of thinking seems immature; hey... that's what *I* get. She believes that all that matters is what she does or what she wants. Guess what? It does... and that's what *I* friggin' get! Her needs are being met... mine aren't! Hold on a sec though... now that I think about it, my needs weren't being met with my previous girl either, or the one before her. Dayum, I GET IT!

Where Is Love? 4

I read some definition of love that said it's our ability to accept someone in spite of their faults; To in fact, embrace them because of their *deficits.*
I say... B·U·L·L·C·R·A·P!

Do not confuse accepting lesser standards with accepting the person. (see pg.148)

How could they ever satisfy or meet any need of mine when they are caught up in their own deficits and I never chose them?
You know what's crazy though, I'm not alone in this type of behavior of allowing myself to be chosen and selected. Most of the guys I know do the same thing, as do the females that I know. But when I get down to it and honestly put some thought into it, I realize it's just me being lazy or better yet, me fearing the work that it takes to find someone who complements me.
I had mentioned these thoughts to my friend Joanne while we were having a discussion of the idea of there being no guarantees in life, but I always opted to the contrary.

Of course, tomorrow isn't promised, but how we work with the time we have does guarantee our happiness within that time. For instance, she is a brilliant young woman that chose to be a nurse.

Chapter 1 - Relationship Reflection

Somewhere Joanne had learned that if she wanted to achieve that goal... she could, as long as she was willing to put in the work that it took. She had been advocating the "no-guarantee" theory, but now I had broken through and showed her that there was a guarantee... it just required effort to ensure it.

In fact, all good things for our souls seem to require the most intense of our efforts. Let's see... a great education, a successful career, the salvation of our souls... so why not our selection for the one we want to trust to nurture, protect, and cherish our hearts? I mean I gotta be ringing some bells in the heads out there.

Ok, so what about some research? We do it for everything else...

You ever take a minute to stop and think about how hard you are willing to push yourself to achieve those things which may only prove satisfactory for a season, when compared to the real needs of your heart? I know you're like, "What the heck are you talking about dude?" I mean, from as far back as I could remember, when I wanted something, I taught myself to go through whatever and suffer however to get it.

All the kids in the hood had nice bikes and I didn't, so I had a choice of going to the nearest suburban town and stealing one, [like so many other kids did], or I could get a paper route and save up. I chose the latter option, but inherent in my choice was a lesson that I could have anything I wanted as long as I was willing to work hard for it.

The catch is that I did this for mostly material goods... or should I say immaterial *things*? I wasn't able to comprehend that this same lesson could be applied to better, more credible achievements in my life. I guess the more intense my desire, the more fear of not succeeding, so the message proved relevant in application to things that I could live without, if all failed.

Perhaps what may have been even more unapparent at that time was the research that I put into concentrating my effort. It remained autonomous, although it was the truest reason for my success in my endeavors. Hmmm... let's really take a look at that.

I hit 17 and the first thing on my noodle was getting my license, but the mechanics of driving weren't naturally developed in me. So what that meant was that I was going to have to find a way to get my driving skills up if I was ever going to get my license.

Chapter 1 - Relationship Reflection

I began by going to someone I trusted and asking them about driving [my uncle Cosmo who drove taxis in NYC] and he agreed to teach me. Cosmo took me into the city and said, "You know, there's only one way to really learn," while pulling to the side of the road.

He stopped, parked, got out, and came around to the passenger side and said, "Get out and drive!"

I was placed in charge of our futures and navigating the outcome of where we were and where we were going. Just like that, I went from having a desire to do something that would make me popular, to doing that very thing and having to be responsible for more than just myself. Relationships are the same way; except we tend to put in less upfront research... in truly unsafe fashion we just hop in and drive!

We have so many expectations of our partners, but we spend no time investigating who those partners are other than just some beautiful woman, or handsome man. In the end, we always find that this selection criterion was not just bogus, but it couldn't possibly guarantee our happiness, because there wasn't any investment in our desires on our part. So how do we break this cycle and rectify our actions? We have to go to the source of the problem.

Using X-Ray Vision... on taking a look inside...

Before we can begin to truly determine whom it is we want to be with, we have to know what we want and even more importantly, we must know who we are, what we have to offer and that we deserve the absolute best. Personally, that was always the zenith of my problem: I thought I wasn't worthy of being loved.

It's critical to make sure that you identify whether you are a person that is trapped in this mindset because it almost guarantees that you will sabotage anything that is good for you. The inexperience of ever being genuinely accepted and loved causes you to think that when it does come your way, it has ulterior meanings.

They couldn't possibly be showing me love because I really don't deserve to be loved. Then what happens is that you end up hurting someone that really doesn't deserve it because it's the displaced anger that you held on to from the previous relationship. This is the infamous baggage that you hear people talk about having when they enter a new relationship.

Additionally, another factor in this formation of self-depravation grows from the constant need to put forth certain images for those that we are closest to. This is especially true for women.

Chapter 1 - Relationship Reflection

Young ladies that may have been in a search for their identities usually will have indulged in some promiscuous behavior. This tends to take place while they are away at school. Once they move back home and are back in a familial social setting where the pressure of being their parents' child has returned, they will start to live their life in a way that their parents might deem acceptable for them.

Now any mistake made in selecting a mate is under such scrutiny that it becomes easier to simply deny yourself the desire to be with someone.

That's not living though, and certainly not honest living, because you are not allowing your heart a chance to express itself. I say constantly that I would rather love, have my heartbroken, get over it and try again and possibly get it broken all over, rather than sit on the sideline wondering what could have happened had I... That's living with regrets, which is a for sure no-no in my life, since it can make the sweetest person undermine the best situations.

I'm not simply suggesting some theoretical perspective... I was the dummy that did this and pushed away one of the sweetest women I ever met in my life. Ms. Joy Tranks. I get sick just thinking of how stupidly I handled our relationship.

Joy was this exceptionally beautiful woman whose path I stumbled across luckily and we began a constant dialogue that made me feel so good that I was ready to throw any hesitancy to the wind. She was one of those rare treasures that was as beautiful in her interior as she was on her exterior.

There was nothing phony about her. She was intelligent and more importantly, she was totally into me.

I recall us meeting for our first date and spending what in all honesty was the best day I had ever spent with any woman. We didn't do anything extreme in terms of the actual activities, but our chemistry and like for each other just made us so comfortable with each other. We both had to yield to the appeal of being together. It was the night I never wanted to end... probably because I knew that deep down I wouldn't know how to handle it later.

We continued for nearly a month with everything going absolutely perfect and she confided how much she liked me and that in fact, she felt herself falling for me. Something in that conversation initiated a change in my behavior towards her.

Chapter 1 - Relationship Reflection

Worse of all, I wasn't conscientious that I felt like that and couldn't recognize myself destroying the bond that I had just worked so hard to establish between us. Yet, hereI was killing us.

I began to tell her little untruths, just to test her reaction to whatever I said and I did it so much she didn't know whether I was kidding or just some twisted, pathological liar.

I gotta be honest, when I couldn't figure out why I was doing all these wrong things, I began to wonder about my mental state because here I was working overtime to destroy a relationship that was so beautiful with a woman that is absolutely incredible and genuinely into me. A woman that was falling in love with me... *oh M G... she's falling in love with me... me! Why me? No one ever loves me! Not my mother, not my mother's mother! I must be friggin crazy... why am I doing this? I don't even want to...* but I couldn't stop!

Finally, one day we were talking about something miniscule and she asked a question of me and before I could even think, I lied to her and was sitting there dumbfounded as to why? I remember thinking and saying to myself, " Hey jackass, you gotta get a grip on this ish, she's already about to tiptoe out the front door... what the hell are you doing?"

Where Is Love? 12

Hell, she had previously warned me that if I did one more deceitful thing... she was gonna leave me! Now you tell me, would any man with a rational mind go on and deliberately respond counter to what was in their best interest and certain to push the woman of their dreams away from them? Of course not.

So what do you think I did?

I went right on and lied to her again and lost her. We both were so devastated because we couldn't believe I had caused all of that pain to her.

A few months later, we talked and she confronted me on my behavior and I broke down in tears and could not explain for the life of me why I had acted in such an ignorant way. We shared such an intimate exchange of how this had affected us both. She made me aware of the fact that regardless of the events that had taken place, she was still in love and willing to stay the course with me as long as I was ready to get myself together. So as desperate as I was to be back with her and as much as I desired to prove to her that I would do right by her, you would probably be 95% certain that "this fool ain't gonna f*^# it up again, he just couldn't!"

Well... I did it again

and I lost her forever!

That particular episode in my life, along with some other events, began to set in motion a period of soul-searching to determine who I was and what kind of man I was. I honestly thought I was a good catch, but now I was questioning myself and worse of all, I had never had any of these bad habits prior to this relationship... so why was I bugging out now?

Up until the last month or so, I have been single for 7 years and abstinent for the last 2 1//2. I can sit here and tell you that I did so as some type of intuition, but I would be lying. I honestly wound up using the time to mature because I saw that there were deficits in my character and I wanted to change and grow. The breaking down of my relationship to JT was enough to damn near push me to my critical meltdown.

Where Is Love?   14

Ladies... please pay attention because this is the answer to your million dollar question on men and our messed up thought process...

Far too many times I have heard women talk ill of some male and complain about his behavior. In fact, I heard it so much I became bothered by it and began to offer my rebuttal to their statements.

{Take a seat ladies, because you really won't like what I am about to share with you, but it's the God's honest truth!}

The deficits you find in most men usually exist for 3 reasons; let's discuss the first of these. Men tend to think and act inappropriately because their mothers allowed them to be taught foolishness, which they idly sat by and saw pounded consistently into that male child's brain; so in essence his momma taught him that!

Let's keep it funky, only a woman can teach a male child how to be sensitive and emotionally expressive. However, if she makes a mockery of his good efforts and intentions, she can destroy his ability to ever be sensitive and cause him to shut down emotionally. This is the second reason you find men full of deficits and incomplete as a person.

Chapter 1 - Relationship Reflection

Women that they get involved with, who have been mistreated previously, tend to hold on to their wounds and usually take out their heartache on the guy that comes along and is good to them. [I will come back to this a bit more in depth a little later.]

Ooowee... I know somebody out there is salty with me right about now, but I have to stay honest with you... just give a brother a few ticks and I will make plenty sense of these thoughts.

REASON 1: Momma, auntie, granny...women raising boys to become men, if you allow that male child to hear, accept, believe cheap, machismo rhetoric, he will eventually act out accordingly. The result will be an inexpressive, emotionally shallow, adult-sized boy.

So how does this happen exactly?

Like in so many families, around the 4th... cookouts are in full swing with everyone sitting around. The boys tend to all huddle around Uncle Joe. You know him.

He's that uncle with the gold-framed, front tooth, reliving his glory days by contaminating these young children with his tales of exploits of fake female conquests: Bringing to life their need to be accepted by him in camaraderie based on being just as shallow and whorish.

Where Is Love? 16

Uncle Joe gets his approval by continuing the disgusting habits that have been taught to him as rites of passage for this particular gathering. While the youth all huddle, Uncle Joe asks, "How many girlfriends you got?" Each young man in turn responds with an answer ranging from the impossible to the truth.
The most bold and brash present the more outrageous fallacies, in hopes of securing the coveted "top dog" spot amongst their peers. **"I got 6 girlfriends Uncle Joe."** "Yeah boy… you just like ya Uncle Joe!"
Again, Uncle Joe = liar, whore, emotionally void, completely shallow, adult-sized boy.

Not only will this youth model the social actions of Uncle Joe, but he may additionally model all of Joe's actions in hopes of "being like Uncle Joe." That can be pretty grim, when you consider that Joe is currently a security guard working overnight in a nursing home. Not to belittle his position, but it reflects how he may not have reached his potential. Especially when you consider that he was Dean's list in an honors program, studying law at Seton Hall… 32 years ago.

REASON *2:* **& *3*** The ladies tend to always want to choose the thug and in their pursuit of one they fail to validate the emotions of the male in front of them.

Chapter 1 - Relationship Reflection   17

Think about it, why should we put our emotions out there when it will only cause us pain? We'd rather shut down!

Are you women out here really considering what it is you are saying? In fact, are you recognizing the magnitude of what you say to us? "Don't be weak, a real man ain't weak..." this is the continuation of a statement told to male children that is the nucleus of unexpressed emotions in men. The utterly disgusting, "boys [and therefore(men)] don't cry!"
Then there is, "I need a man with some thug in him, cuz if he too nice, he don't have no spine."

We interpret this as... "I need to be not so attentive, or sensitive... actually a bit more arrogant, shallow... I shouldn't let her see that I realize her worth in my life. If I do, she will start to try to emasculate me. She won't trust my ability to lead us and will constantly question my judgment."

I need to know! Do you women really know what a thug is, from our perspective? He *is* the one that goes upside your head. He *is* the one that disregards your feelings, by staying out all night and not calling. He *is* concerned with what he desires and thinks you are here to fulfill his needs.

Where Is Love?   18

He *is* not about handling his business like a man ought to... he searches for the short cuts always! He doesn't fear anything, except maybe a more unscrupulous thug.

FYI: ONLY A WOMAN CAN TEACH A BOY TO BE A COMPLETE MAN

As a reference to how this process usually goes awry, I would like to introduce you all to Deonte Stahl. This is of course a dummy name to protect the identity of a dummy I used to consider to be my best friend... my brother from another mother in fact.

D is a classic presentation of the boy hiding in a man's body that will never grow up. From the time he was a boy, his mother had been babying him by taking care of everything, rather than teaching him to be responsible for himself. I'm talking chores, earning his own money, buying incidentals like comic books, bike inner tubes, sneakers, etc.: the things that most little boys learn to save up for. This boy wanted for absolutely nothing!

Her intentions were to show her son that she loves and cherishes him.

She didn't want him to experience the hardships of life, which had been a constant part of her own childhood. She was attempting to give him a better life than the one that she had experienced growing up in.

Chapter 1 - Relationship Reflection

That's admirable and every parent should aspire to such noble intentions, but it must be tempered with restraint so that the regular lessons of becoming a productive member of society can be taught and learned.

As a result of the unintentional coddling, Deonte never did the dishes, he never cleaned his room, he never did his laundry, he never paid his own bills, HE NEVER HAD ANY CHORES! When his father attempted to step in and make him do these things, D knew to simply wait his father out and his mom would eventually do it for him.

In fact, this process continued and followed him into adulthood. Up until about 6 years ago, when he got married, his mom was still *paying for his haircuts*!

No, I'm not kidding, here was a 30+ year old man, letting his mother spring for his haircuts and doing his laundry weekly. That is absolutely crazy!

He was my roommate several times and these deficits always arose and I ended up being his daddy all the time. When he finally got married, nothing had changed. He was still the same boy, but in a 6'5" body... and his poor wife suffers continually with the boy that will never become a man. The unwillingness to grow up in him actually began to affect other segments of his life.

Where Is Love?   20

Deonte Stahl's inability to pay rent on time and in full, paying his share of the energy or cable bills, his inability to contribute to the bills associated with his very own partnership, all were a direct result of his tendency to play the boy in any and all adult situations. It was his immature way of ducking the pressure of making adult decisions and committing to them. This became such an ordeal that it pushed away all of his male friends... I mean lifelong buddies... locked together... since day-care and VBS!

We tried to hold on and teach him to embrace being more mature as a man, but we were always having our feelings slighted or taken advantage of, so it just became too much to bare anymore.

This next portion really is an indirect appeal to men all across the nation to learn to change and present models of manhood, especially when you look at the state of the family today and see the violence that has become a norm in far too many neighborhoods, directly related to the lack of men in the lives of those very youth. When there is no clear example of what a man is supposed to look, think, act like, male children REMAIN adult-sized boys. These boys grow up to be *incomplete* men.

Chapter 1 - Relationship Reflection

In their incomplete state, they are left to pick from one of three possibilities for a partner. They can want a woman and end up choosing a girl, or they can opt to look for their own in-home clone of their mother, or they can choose a woman.

The first possibility is not just the easiest, but also the most popular because most men don't even realize the difference between a woman and a girl. The fact that she cooks and cleans DOES NOT make her a woman and if a woman opts to not be domesticated, that DOES NOT mean she isn't a woman.

However, too many men use this as the criteria for determining a "real" woman. This faulty criterion can create within too many men a longing for them to be nurtured again, so many look for the in-home remake/clone of their mother. They miss the nurturing and think that a good relationship is based on mothering.

[A] The choice of the girl represents the man's fear of being challenged and engaged... he believes everything will go his way, even though he will most often suffer most in this scenario, because if he starts to mature and she remains in the state he found her in, they obviously will not be complementary to each other.

Where Is Love?

This is the man supposedly presenting his independence.

[B] The choice of the mother-clone represents the man's fear of growing into maturity and engaging in the process of decision-making... he is willing to let someone else be responsible for all the daily nuances that are part of a regular adult routine.

He wants the luxury of being able to SELECT which decisions he should make. These most likely will be the things he feels strongest partaking in, economic activities [his job and hobbies].

This tends to work well when the woman is of a mindset wherein, she doesn't have to answer the challenge of being able to make her own money. She'll trade her economic independence for a life of domestication because she believes in [the] "way to his heart is through his stomach" theory.

The problem with both of these is that he doesn't respect either woman. They simply occupy functions that he needs completed in his daily life.

[C] The last choice represents the man's ability to address his heart based on his sincere belief in what should naturally occur, even if he will end up shortchanging a great woman.

Chapter 1 - Relationship Reflection

You see, most men deal with a difficulty of recognizing the difference between a woman and a girl. To assist us all in a clear understanding, I am going to provide an outline of attributes that define **MY** idea of a woman. My idea people... I don't want anyone going crazy on me; this is my idea!

1] A woman is a female that handles her business in such a way as to obtain a professional background that allows her to be able to not simply enter, but advance and prosper in the corporate world.

I need to know that if we have worked hard to build an empire that it won't simply collapse because she has no skills to provide for my babies and herself. *Good women are prepared.*

2] A woman understands the need to maintain her own individuality, even though she has fallen in love. Too often this is a major problem in relationships. The woman falls in love and the man becomes her main focus, and if she is not careful... her only focus.

This begins her tendency to possibly violate his privacy by rifling through his pockets.

Ladies, by no means is any man pleased by a woman that snoops through his things. If you ask your man about something, then be loyal enough to believe his response.

Where Is Love?   24

That is... **unless** he is giving you a reason to not believe in him. If it reaches that point...LEAVE him!

Queens shouldn't come off their thrones!

By that I mean, don't start lowering yourself by acting in ways that are beneath you. And my brothers, be men of your word. Kings lead kingdoms... once you recognize the beauty in a woman that is willing to follow your lead, you must be aware of the ability to abuse that woman if you lead by other than noble ways and actions.

Good men don't stoop and good women don't snoop.

3] A woman is a motivator that is clever enough to move her man towards his greatness and have him embrace the best in himself, while having him believe that it was his doing of his own accord. She is interested in the end result... the great man that she knows is in him.

Good women create great men.

4] A woman is the female that has the remedy for all of her man's woes. She uses all of her skills to establish a realm of peace. In the Chinese language, the character for the word Peace is a house with a woman in it.

Chapter 1 - Relationship Reflection

This is such a poignant observation, hidden in the etymology of a word. Considering this, any honest man that has enjoyed true joy and peace will probably acknowledge that peace came from a woman, whether direct or roundabout. *Good women bring about peace.*

5] A woman is a female that is unafraid to embrace her power to nurture. This is her presentation of her public display of affection, which soon enough will become the basis for her skills as a mother.

This is such an attractive quality in a woman, because it shows men her unselfishness and willingness to put others ahead of herself. *Good women are unselfish and sacrifice for those they love.*

6] A woman is a female that conducts herself in a manner becoming of reverence and respect. She realizes that all eyes are on her and she accepts her role as a model for sophisticated womanhood. *Good women carry themselves as queens.*

7] A woman is a female that knows how to reinvent herself constantly. Men tend to place a high value on visceral attraction from what they see. A woman understands that she needs to be her man's eye candy.

Where Is Love? 26

Does this mean she is dressing like a model all day, everyday... no.

But she draws him into her, by using all her attributes, because she wants to stimulate his attraction to her.

Good women make their men want them.

Now I don't want any ladies running up to me and wanting to kill me... so for a point of clarity, when I am presenting these attributes, they take into account that we are talking about a good man.

8] A woman is intelligent. She understands how to use her thoughts to foster a strong bond between her and others. She makes use of her mental capacity in ways that enhance her value and present her as someone to be reverenced. *A good woman is smart.*

9] A woman is calm. She knows that it's best to remain even-tempered in all situations, so that she can react proactively. Her peace solicits the peace in others.

A good woman perpetuates peace.

10] A woman possesses money-management skills... she knows how to stretch today's dollar until tomorrow's need.

Chapter 1 - Relationship Reflection

She realizes that even though certain purchases could be made right now, its best that she invest time in looking for value for her money, because her family benefits. *A good woman is thrifty.*

11] And finally, a woman is a female that conducts herself as a lady in public, but is an absolute freak in private. This allows her mate to experience variation in the range of his emotions, which he will find most exhilarating. She is proving that submission is not a bad thing and that she is open to anything, as long as it's with her man.

A good woman is multifaceted.

7-8 minutes of convo is all it takes... the Golden moment...

About a year ago, I was having a sit down to announce to some ladies that I was writing this book. They were enthusiastic and proceeded to ask me for a few gems from the book. I said, " well it seems to me that the most appropriate thing I can share with you is an understanding of how men tend to communicate." The ladies became extremely vocal, validating my choice of discussion with cheers and shrieks of excitement.

I asked them to give me examples of how they thought men communicated.

One of the ladies said, "I think that most men tend to suppress everything of importance. They fail to recognize the pivotal moments of talking. It's like they despise having to share what's going on inside themselves." I smiled and acknowledged the depth of her commentary by remarking, "Exactly."
Ladies, it's important to get an understanding of why men communicate, well... actually lack the ability to communicate to your satisfaction.

It's a fact that far too many of our families are lead by a single woman that works multiple jobs to support children that she created with some male that has chosen to shun his responsibility.

As a result of her need to generate enough income to handle all the obligations alone, she has to sacrifice the quality time that she would prefer to spend with her children. Certain lessons of life are left untaught because there simply isn't any time. In the case of her male children, a lack of sensitivity and communication skills is the deficit that results. If anything is taught, it's a sense of the importance of earning money at all opportunities and not being anything like their daddy. After all, he was just into "sweet-talking" her and "making these babies" and then "up and leaving."

Chapter 1 - Relationship Reflection

She doesn't even want to create a soft man... her resentment for the father will soon become the child's resentment for women, as he is unable to accurately interpret why she is always yelling at him. At a time when he needs to be developing his emotional stability and ability to communicate, she is shutting him down emotionally, so how is he supposed to learn what he needs to be an emotionally complete man from this emotionally shattered woman?

Believe it or not, this is far too commonplace for young men of all races, and explains the communication deficit in men across the nation.

In an effort to assist all of the relationships that suffer from this deficit, I am going to share techniques of communication that will enhance how each partner engages the other.

The first thing to recognize in meeting anyone of the opposite sex is your window of opportunity for talking to that person. There is something called the "Golden moment", when complete strangers have a chance wherein they can communicate at an optimum level. For example, you walk past someone and notice that the person is definitely to your liking.

Where Is Love?

In that first 10 seconds, your eyes lock and you both smile. At that moment, you should engage in your conversation, but most often people allow this moment to escape and as the window closes, the courage to reveal your intentions diminishes. Now let's say that you choose to speak, the conversation should reveal the potential of the couple within 7 – 8 minutes. Even so, please keep in mind that during any conversation, the average man has an attention span of 15 words per sentence.

Ladies if you are going to say anything of importance, that message must be conveyed in less than ten words, as the first 9 are the most important; they are the words that are *actually* heard.

This critical 7 – 8 minutes will allow each party to determine the value of the other and make an assessment of how that person can be complementary to their life. It allows them to choose whether this person is to be seriously pursued or whether to pull back and refrain from investing any more time in the exchange. In those 7 – 8 minutes, a man can determine whether he is addressing a woman or a girl, which also explains why so many men avoid talking.

Chapter 1 - Relationship Reflection

Too many men don't want the responsibility of knowing the maturity level of the person they are engaging, because it directly reflects on their own requirement for successfully engaging in any social exchange with that person. Additionally, it exposes the inherent nastiness of this old hawk preying on an innocent young chick if his intent is other then noble. You ever look around and notice men way too old, all wrapped up in some 17 year old; you start thinking, how the heck does that happen. Well, he doesn't do much talking, or he would instantly recognize that this is a child, unless he is mentally immature. In which case, he would prefer to not allow his deficit to be discovered, especially if he is married... but I will get into that one in more detail a bit later! [see pg.89]

Men come from the dungeon and women come from somewhere else...

So let's suppose that we actually come from opposing points of existence... of course women would come from somewhere of a higher plateau and men would come from the dungeon. Just this starting difference illustrates how vast of a difference there is in the motives of engaging each other.

Where Is Love?
32

Although she can start out with pure intentions of befriending him and letting things progress from there, as to where NO MAN EVER HAS the intention of STARTING OUT AS A FRIEND! This doesn't mean that a man doesn't want his lady to be his best friend, but his intentions for initially addressing her were not to build a friendship.

The need to conquer the chase will allow him to adapt and endure the lengthy process of establishing a friendship first, but only if he thinks he may at some future date be able to convince her to change her view of him and see him as a potential mate or he loses his interest in her romantically. Ladies, you all probably think that is really foul, but you have to understand how a male interprets the need to establish an emotional tie to someone.

A male tends to view emotionally connecting to someone as the exposure of a weakness in himself, as this can alter his ability to act freely if the object of his affection is threatened or harmed. You may note that a significant amount of men excel in their careers when they ignore the development of their socialization in their personal life.

Chapter 1 - Relationship Reflection

Usually men need a great woman to be active in their lives in order to excel in all the other parts of their lives.

This woman is the one who crosses the boundaries of his emotional stability and invests in intertwining with his heart for a pure purpose of loving him. In exchange, his loyalty to her reaches a level of invulnerability because he appreciates that she can cultivate and unlock all the hidden potential he has for greatness. Recall the statement, "Behind every good man is a great woman!" Again, this is referring to a complete man who is mature and understands the enhanced value of his life because of that specific woman that he chose, who put her all into him.

He should want to go to any ends required to make sure that she knows that he finds her to be an invaluable part of his existence.

Destroying the myth of the Gold-Digger...

Ok... I'm sitting in the presence of a group of young men. One of the youth makes a statement. *"Yeah, she must be crazy! I ain't giving a bitch shit!"* Of course, the teacher and father in me, jumps to action. If ever there was an opportunity for a teaching intervention that can change the mentality of our society, this was certainly mine. Trust that I wasn't going to waste it!

Where Is Love?

First the correction..."*Young man... do you recognize that I am a **grown man** sitting in your presence?*" "*Oh... yeah... my bad. I didn't mean to disrespect you. I'm just saying how it is with these bi... I mean chicks. You know what I mean? They always want shit!*"

"*Let's begin at addressing them properly... they aren't bitches, chicks, or any of the vast other disparaging terms that you young men tend to use to describe them. They create life. They aren't here to get smashed, taxed, hit, waxed, banged, pounded, ripped or fucked. Love doesn't hurt, yet your description of the most sacred physical representation of love between us, does not represent love at all, but rather sounds like the most brutal of atrocities. Please remember she creates life.*"

"*And what is that supposed to mean? Just cuz a chick can get pregnant, I am supposed to worship the ground she walks on?*" "*Not worship, but celebrate. Walk with me for a moment. Young king... I called you that because you most have presented the austerity of the ancient rulers, which you and I came from. Great rulers that were doing things at the age of 12 that the current government cannot accept without challenge.*

Chapter 1 - Relationship Reflection

The idea of elected representation, democracy, the union of states... are all ideologies from the minds of past teenagers in power. If men were that great, then the women that provide the continuation of their genius through the birthing of their heirs, should prove equally worthy of reverence. They must be at the very least, equally powerful." **The young brothers sat in silence considering what I had just said. I decided to continue.**

"Young kings, I need to teach you about the danger of believing in myths and propagandas. Perhaps the one that is most significant in your life is the myth of the gold digger." "But a myth is like a lie told to give a message to the listener, gold diggers are real. I see them all the time!" " I know you have grown up believing that a woman that shows her man that she needs things is supposed to be undesirable."

"I want to ask you all, who is responsible for the financial well-being of the family... the mother or the father?" "The man is supposed to take care of his family. God gave him the job of being the provider." "I couldn't have stated that any better if I had tried; you both additionally said that God **placed** *man in that position. So what is a provider... isn't he the one that is responsible for acquiring the financial means necessary to take care of the essential needs of his family?*

A roof over their head, clothes on their back, food in their belly, school supplies for education, a bed to rest on, shoes on their feet, etc.

When I was a youth about your age, my grandma taught me the importance of realizing that anyone that I seriously considered to be my girlfriend, had the potential to end up my wife. During the courtship, everything should be done in such a manner as to show to my mate that I would be a great provider to her. In essence, it's the practice run for being in a marriage.

Men of that time always knew it was their responsibility to take care of their women; they saw it as an honor and a mark of their manhood. They took pride in doing so because they knew that it gave their family confidence in their abilities as a man.

With the coming of female suffrage and female independence, this role of the man became fairly obsolete. Women did not want to be seen as needing anyone to do for them, and men who disagreed with the movement, used it as an excuse to drop the ball with regards to them fulfilling their responsibilities. Soon an old term resurfaced, but the reference had been significantly modified to have a negative connotation and it also was given a sexual component.

Chapter 1 - Relationship Reflection

Gold Digger – originally a term that embodied the spirit of entrepreneurial ship – male entrepreneurial ship! These men were seen as the rugged go-getters that forged ahead to areas uncharted in search of resources that could allow them to better take care of their families. Now the very same term is being used to signify an aggressive person, woman in particular, that would do anything to get someone else to give them what they need. This one word has signally emasculated the provider role of man. As men grew more embarrassed by their acceptance of the ideology, they relinquished more of their responsibility. There is no such thing as a gold digger... its simply man's way of shucking off his responsibility to act as a provider." "But sir, that's cool if you are married. We ain't married to these girls!" "Remember what I said though, the courtship is the practice stage. But let's get away from that.

Let's take a typical situation. You become involved with a young lady. You think she's gorgeous and she has shown you that she possesses all the qualities that you have been searching for in a partner. The two of you start to hang out quite often. She has a job and takes very good care of herself.

Where Is Love?   38

You grow accustomed to always seeing her at her best: hair done, nails painted and clothing stylish. Six months pass and she loses her job as cutbacks force her employer to let go of his newest employees. She becomes very depressed because she is so used to always taking care of herself [an example of her independence]. She has always been generous to you, but she honestly does not expect you to do anything. You notice that she hasn't been coming around as much though.

You call her and she tells you she is ok, but she hasn't really been in the mood to be around people. You decide to pay her an unannounced visit just to cheer her up. When you get to her house, you hear a woman yelling about money. You peek through the window and see her crying, but you are in shock. She looks nothing like the girl you know.

She looks like she hasn't been taking care of herself, and she has lost noticeable weight. You decide not to knock, to spare her the embarrassment. She happens to peer out the window and sees you leaving.

Now, if she were to run out the door and explain what you saw and overheard and tell you that she needs money to pay her share of the rent... is she a gold digger? Do you feel obligated to take care of her?"

Chapter 1 - Relationship Reflection

"Wow, you are so right big bruh. I never thought of it like that. My grandma always says that we are taking that girl away from her dad, so we need to do as good a job as he does. You are really putting it into an example that I understand now."

Just an example of what we can accomplish when we reach out to these babies and invest in them. I could have walked by like everyone else, but they needed to know the truth and they needed to see a father figure explain the role of being a man, so that they can assess, learn, and implement it.

Once again, before this section ends...

there is

NO SUCH

THING AS

A

GOLD DIGGER!

Where Is Love?   40

Chapter 2 – Breaking Down Barriers

Young sapling... 'tis the early morn when I most notice thee shedding off the weight of the frost and adjusting as the sun's rays prepare ye to stand. –
Prose

Young boys & their things; old men & their questions (they talk that way because that's the best form of communication they can muster)...

Probably the best place to begin this chapter would be to have you think of yourself sitting in front of your computer. You're feeling lonely and about to go on one of those hook-up sites like Tagged, BPM, or E Harmony.

You read the various profiles and discover that women usually say too little **or** way too much. They speak about their children, their spirituality, their family, and friends. After you have met quite a few women through this process, they start to migrate towards you or steer clear of you.

That flow of direction usually stems from how your profile is written. This is where the disparity amongst men begins. The more exceptional men can describe themselves in emotional terms that describe and capture the essence of who they are.

Where Is Love?   42

All other men follow the normal route; they talk about their things if they are young and if they are older, they probe you to death with defensive questions. I chose this context to illustrate the point, because this behavior is always displayed during the initial dialogue of a first meeting between a man and woman.

Take for instance 19-year-old Candace and 20-year-old Angelo. Both attend college at Rutgers University in New Brunswick, NJ. Both come from the homes of affluent African American families. Both have identical backgrounds, as far as job experience, social interaction and education.

While registering for classes on the first day of school, they meet in the Student Activities building. *"Hey, you have a lot of books there. Let me help you." "It's ok. I've got them."* **One book starts to fall; Angelo catches the book in midair.** *"You got them hungh?" "Well, thanks... I'm Candace."* *"Angelo Aurelius Jackson the 3rd. You probably noticed the mid-air catch from this month's ESPN magazine: Only my 2nd article of the season, singing the praises of Rutgers' second year, All American receiver and legend in the making. With all of those books, you are certainly going to need a ride and my 370z might be just what doctor Angelo ordered.*

Chapter 2 - Breaking Down Barriers

Well... that's after you have a little personal soiree at my penthouse suite in my Jacuzzi tub."

"My God, it never stops does it?" "What?" "You boys talking about your things. Is that supposed to woo me or something, or perhaps your possessions have the power to turn me into an absolute whore; even worse, a whore that likes your things, and not you. Why would you even want someone like that... is that the best you can do Angelo?"

The words reverberated in his mind as he gave thought to her every syllable. He now found himself in a deep, meditative state considering exactly why he had spoken to the lovely young woman in such a way. He knew that she was a woman of quality and that she certainly wasn't the chicken-head type. Why had he talked down to her as though she should accept his materialistic, machismo rap? All he could think of was the lost of her and it ached him to his soul.

Meet Mr. Boreaugard Jenkins. He is a throwback to the days of the Mack. To him the ways of the pimp are like religion in modern day churches. Please don't tell him a damn thing about his pimping! For the last week or so, Boreaugard has developed a hankering for Ms. Alice, the retired school teacher that opened up Evan's diner.

Where Is Love?   44

Each evening he strolls in and cajoles her in his best pomposity. This evening, he is in rare form.

"Listen here pretty brown, woman was created to please man. and some men are way more man than others, so they need more women. Now to the man who ain't a natural pimp, these women would get out of line because he don't know how to lay his smack down. Me, I am the originator and innovator. from the snakes on my feet to the bills in my gator. Gigantic player, the all day I ever lay ya. Mouth so full of smack, three times make ya jump back from the diamond in the back. sun-roofed top, digging the scene with my gangster lean... woo ooo ooo CHURCH! "

"Now Mr. Boreaugard, how many times have you come in here and laid that ole tired rap down on me?" "Well a few." "And how many times has that tired ole rap worked for you?" "Well none yet, but that was because I was warming you up real good. No biscuit ever got et without the buttering up. You got to come to realize. why wouldn't an ole gal like you want a pimp like myself? I mean, with no me in ya life, it must get pretty empty, don't it?" "Man, are you serious? You old fools and your questions!"

Chapter 2 - Breaking Down Barriers

These complaints signify a problem that I recognized in men across a range of years, ever since I began to undertake this endeavor. I don't know how many times I have heard women complain about this specific issue and I felt embarrassed by the stories that they shared about how men addressed them during various conversations.

As I continued to pay attention to this problem, a pattern began to emerge; the young boys had a distinct style of how they approached girls. They always wanted to skip pass the real discussion of who they were and go to what they owned. Their property was put in place of their character. The value of their materials was constantly being paraded as their personal invite to why they should be desired and at the end of the day, it's as though they didn't even realize the folly of this practice.

This baffled me at first and I had to spend time trying to assess the rationale for this behavior; finally, it came to me. This was the appropriate guise for anyone still trying to find his identity. Usually, young fellas struggle through their young adult years trying to learn who they are, what they are here to do, and how best to achieve their goals.

Because they haven't truly learned to value themselves, they opt to acquire *things* that have a high value in our society and then past those off as *their* worth.

It's actually a logical way to see themselves, as the thesis of their world is the acquisition of all things blingy and expensive, at any cost, for the sole purpose of showing off. How perfect of a fit is that?

Consider that we are now seeing the second generation of youth that have grown up in a single parent or no-parent home as a standard. These parents that are in the home, are either too young & inexperienced or too old to be able to appropriately care for and discipline today's youth. This is the origin of the deficit that exists in the youth of today, especially the males.

With no one available to invest the necessary time to teach him to first value himself, how will he ever acquire a sense of his worth, an appreciation of him "self"? Additionally, certain lessons of life may never be imparted, such as a need to be sensitive, a need to be gentle and a need to be compassionate.

The mother usually teaches these lessons since she is essentially the standard by which he will learn to give affection to a woman.

Chapter 2 - Breaking Down Barriers

Only a woman can fully teach a male to appreciate the ways in which she needs to be treated: mostly because she knows the rationales for why a woman desires to be engaged in a genteel manner. A young male needs to obtain an understanding of how to value a woman early on, so that he can learn how to appreciate himself. He has no idea what she requires of him, and in essence has no idea what a man is made of.

He is incomplete and has only encountered the masculine side of life: power, acquisition, conquest and appearance. He needs to embrace the feminine side of life: chastity, verbiage, emotions and intimacy. This is the rationale behind most women's decision to date a man that loves his mother. There is a hope that he has received these lessons and knows how to interact with a woman accordingly.

Recently, a good friend of mine, Bailey, found herself intrigued by a young man that for all outward appearances, seemed to have it all together. She began to call him regularly and they exchanged dialogue; it wasn't at a depth that stimulated her. Bailey came to me for advice and from day one I said to, "tell him what you want; be precise, because we [men] can be very naive."

Where Is Love?

So of course, she left and they talked and the issue of what she wants out of the union popped up and she said, "Whatever you want." I wanted to reach out and bite her when she told me that, because my friend is typical of so many wonderful women that end up on the short-end of the stick because they fear being direct will push a man away.

You have just read an example of the typical dialogue coming out of young and old mouths...

Ladies, BE PRECISE!

Tell him what YOU want damn it! Of course, the situation for Bailey has continued downhill with this dude. I told her it would because he is a boy in a man's body, afraid to reach out and connect with a woman for fear that he will lose control of his heart. He can never satisfy her desire as a companion and mate.

Furthermore, my friend is the type of woman that has grown up in the hood with all the coolest dudes taking her under their wing. We all see Bailey as our lil sister, and any guy wanting her, has to deal with us as well. This is often far too intimidating and guys shy away. So my friend has taken to not quite talking about her social surrounding. Again, I have told her, "Don't cloak anything for a guy. You tell him and let him deal with it.

Chapter 2 - Breaking Down Barriers

We were here before him and will be here after him, so he has to get over that! It shouldn't matter if his esteem is healthy and he has no ill-intent."

In this case, he has been dropping little, so-called playful remarks about all the guys being around her, how late she hangs out and all of the things that come out of the mouth of someone who wants to control you. This being the pink phase of engaging each other, she is ready to compromise and yield to his need.

BUT WHAT ABOUT YOUR FRIGGIN' NEEDS?

Hear me well ladies... under no circumstances should you ever be willing to compromise for any man that hasn't made a sacrifice for you first. He needs to show nobility, before he deserves compromise. At the same time, you must show grace, so as to create a comfort zone where he can be free to put his heart on display. ***Never prioritize someone that doesn't put you first!***

What's crazy is how all of this stems from that initial dialogue between you; if he can't talk, then it becomes a simple choice. You will either be willing to teach him to communicate and that means accepting all of the faults that will come with him learning.

Where Is Love?   50

If he has gone this far without those skills, it will take some time and consistency on both your parts to assist him in successfully learning to communicate effectively. Of course the easier choice may be, you simply are not willing... and that's perfectly fine too.

Either way the decision should be an easy one... *if* you have practiced chapter one's advice and can remember the 80-20 rule. If this person gives you 80% of what you feel you need in a relationship, then he is most likely worth the investment of your effort in assisting him in learning those skills that can assure him of inevitably providing the remaining twenty.

On pg.23, I took the time to define my ideal woman, so in an effort to balance things out, I want to provide a list of attributes that are essential to defining a man.

1] A man is a male that understands and embraces his responsibility as the provider for his home. He seeks to conduct himself in business in such a way as to provide his children with an image of the proper role of a father and additionally lay the foundation for their security.

His purpose should not simply be to bring in enough to survive, but enough to address all needs of his family and most desires. This maintains the comfort of home and strengthens his leadership.

Chapter 2 - Breaking Down Barriers

He needs to have worked hard and built an empire that won't simply collapse should he pass, so that all she has to do is maintain it. *Good men are providers.*

2] A man understands the need to assist his woman in maintaining her own individuality, even though she has fallen in love. Too often this is a major problem in relationships. The man sees his woman falling in love and sees that he has become her main focus and in fact... her only focus! He must recognize that this causes her to shrivel up because she is no longer maintaining her autonomy and the camaraderie of hanging with her peers. This is critical as she gains most of her reference of social skills that draw him into her, through this socialization.

By establishing a line of trust for her with her friends, he shows her how to trust in him wholeheartedly and prevents possible violations of his privacy. Men, by no means is it acceptable for a woman to snoop through your things. If you ask your woman to not rifle through your things, then be honest enough to address this behavior, **unless** you are giving her a reason to not believe in you. If she does violate you, it is not cute...LEAVE her!

Kings lead Kingdoms!

Where Is Love?   52

By that I mean, don't start carrying yourself in ways that are not noble, that won't enhance your reputation and that do not encourage your respect.

My brothers, realize that these noble acts shouldn't be regarded as some fantastic newness in man, but rather, sleeping kings returning to their former greatness.

Kings lead kingdoms... once you recognize the power you have as the leader of your home, you must constantly walk a path that parallels your movements. *Good men help their women to remain loyal*, by being someone that she can revere.

3] A man is an entrepreneur that is innovative enough to move towards his greatness and works hard to secure the best in himself. Even though he does this of his own volition, he knows that it his woman that will pull his greatness to the surface and have him achieve his dreams. *Good men work with their woman to cultivate, nourish and turn themselves into great men.*

4] A man is the male that has the remedy for all of his woman's woes. He is her friend, comforter and confidant. He uses all of his skills and resources to establish a foundation of absolute security.

Chapter 2 - Breaking Down Barriers
53

In any relationship, the woman is seeking security, which goes far beyond just the financial connotation, but extends to him serving as her rock against any hardships. If it is non-existent, then she need not be there, as he is not meeting the main motivation for her participation.

Any honest woman that has enjoyed true security will probably acknowledge that feeling came from the efforts that her man set forth, whether direct or roundabout. *Good men give security.*

5] A man is a male that conducts himself in a manner becoming of reverence and respect. He realizes that all eyes are on him and he accepts his role as a model for distinguished manhood. *Good men carry themselves as Kings.*

6] A man is a male that is unafraid to embrace his power to lead. This is his presentation of his public display of strength, which soon enough will become the basis for his skills as a father. This is such an attractive quality in a man, because it shows women his discipline and willingness to sacrifice himself for the well being of everyone else. *Good men are disciplined and sacrifice for those they love.*

Where Is Love?

7] A man is a male that knows how to rejuvenate himself constantly. Women tend to place a high value on their man's ability to provide them with refreshing experiences. No woman wants to fall in the humdrum of a normal routine, and even when this occurs, a man knows how to put the fire back into the relationship. A man understands that he needs to be the flame of passion that ignites his woman's soul. Does this mean he looks like he just stepped out of the pages of GQ? Could be, but it goes deeper... to his core; it's the positive attitude that he projects. He strengthens her faith in him, by using all his attributes to better their union, because he wants to lead. *Good men make their women have faith in them.*

Now I don't want any men running up to me and wanting to kill me... so for a point of clarity, when I am presenting these attributes, they take into account that we are talking about a good woman.

8] A man is intelligent. He understands the power of using his thoughts in a way that creates the state of being that he wants to exist. He establishes his allies by their appreciation of his mental capabilities.

Chapter 2 - Breaking Down Barriers

He pushes the edges of his creative and entrepreneurial skills to develop plans that allow him to give his family a great life and earn him admiration as a man of action. *A good man is always thinking and devising better plans to maximize his potential.*

9] A man is composed. He knows nothing should ever be undertaken in a rush, as this promotes mistakes. He realizes that being proactive in all situations, affords him the advantage of being prepared for the worse. By always remaining composed, those around him are always effortlessly put at ease, because they rely on him to be in control. *A good man masters his self-control.*

10] A man possesses the ability to make money... he knows how to create a financial niche today that will allow him to earn from now until tomorrow. He realizes that certain sacrifices must be made right now, as a method of investing for the future of his family. A complete future that takes into account the recreational and social needs, as well as the essential needs. *A good man is crafty.*

11] And lastly, a man is a male that carries himself as a gentleman in public, a knight when with his family, but the ultimate lover in private. This allows his mate to experience the gamut of his emotions and his differing stages of being, which stimulates her in every way.

Where Is Love?   56

By risking his emotions and sharing everything with her, he assures himself of her loyalty. This is stimulating as it electrifies a woman by showing her that there are no boundaries to what he can achieve for her. He is proving that if she is willing to follow his lead, he will take care of her every need.

A good man keeps his word.

Sharing your emotional state... the rite that binds!

Reciprocity should become the physical manifestation of a man's appreciation for his woman's role in his life.

Here's an added gem for my brothers, if you can remember to add communication of your inner thoughts in collaboration with your physical actions at this point in your relationship, you will create a reinforcing bond that will bind her to you in a way that you had not thought was possible.

With all that you are doing, you expect that she should **KNOW** how you love and appreciate her... but if that is really what you feel, simply give the extra effort and tell her as well as showing her. How else will she know; recall what happens when we ASSUME = We make an ass (of) u (&) me!

Chapter 2 - Breaking Down Barriers   57

Men we need to learn how to consider the whole picture, not just our role in it... we have to start considering all the roles of our family and the contributions that will be required from each to make the family progress successfully. When this has all come together, we should first remember God that has smiled on us and allowed this to happen and give him our thanks. We should follow that by doing the same to the woman in our life that was God's tool in creating this emotional base in our existence. It's true... she is your rib!

Gentlemen consider this, in the essential continuity of your happiness, how much is it worth to you to invest in participating in a genuine ritual of letting her know that you recognize her worth and are thankful for her contribution? Seeing as how she brought you that happiness, why would she jeopardize it when you choose to share your intimate thoughts on her value? If she doesn't deserve to know this secret, then who does? Imagine thinking such thoughts, but never letting them have expression... that's absolutely ridiculous!

Men can be so ignorant when it comes to understanding that this is a wise investment in maintaining her contribution.

Where Is Love?   58

If she feels appreciated, she is going to not simply continue to go hard for the success of the relationship, but she is going to increase her efforts and teach your children to follow her role as well. This more than anything else will become the foundation for how they address the world. Having seen a strong man lead and an even stronger woman allow the man to lead the family gives the children concrete examples of their eventual roles as adults and prepares them to think ahead.

Women have it on point when they say that a man should know their emotional state without words.

This is a point of consideration for the men... a jewel of sorts, if you are willing to truly accept your responsibility with regard to what I am about to share. A significant portion of the women of the world tends to get into debates with their mate and the subject of discussion usually centers on his inability to discern her emotional needs. They honestly ***expect*** their man to be able to recognize that something is troubling them, even though they haven't said a word.

Now most men, playing the simpleton, will poke fun at their mate by saying, "How can I possibly figure out what's bothering you, when you never told me?

Chapter 2 - Breaking Down Barriers

Do I look like I read minds?" In the same vein, he just finished telling her how he thinks something serious is going on with his friend at work, because the friend is usually outspoken, but has been very quiet as of late. *If you know all of that about a colleague at work, then why not the person you claim to love most of all* in this world? She is looking at you and saying, "Hell yes... I expect you to know my needs just like you know his, after all, you are f-ing me; you only *work* with him!"

Do you know that when **we** (men) cop out and act as though **we** are incapable of doing this, **we** start shredding our women's confidence in us? We are their superheroes... recall that we have come in and taken the role that their father used to occupy in their lives. We have promised everything under the sun, but now want an easy way out of keeping our word. It's a failure to accept our obligation to establish an emotional tie to our ladies that drive us to neglect developing this skill within ourselves.

It's in the same line of thinking as the previous section... who more deserves this effort from you, than the person who most contributes to your happiness and completion as a man? Men are supposed to be the leaders of their households.

Where Is Love?

I don't mean that as a tyrant or totalitarian... I mean that in the way that God intended man's proper role as the leader of his family.

Too often men are demanding that their women follow everything they ask, but the men don't provide that example at all. By ignoring your pride and the foolish lessons of love that you originally considered as relevant, you learn that it is so much more important to create a bond with your mate. How much more valuable is she to you, when she can anticipate your needs without any utterance from you. It is beyond satisfying; being the recipient of unselfish attention that came based solely on your need, without you ever saying a word. It leaves you in a state of wonderment and additionally provides proof that this woman cherishes you... she pays attention to you, even when you may think she doesn't.

It's like when you were a little child. Mama would walk into the room with some fresh-cooked soup and tell you to sit up and eat it. Somehow, you were so ready for it, even though you hadn't even had an inkling of a thought towards eating. How had she known?

Chapter 2 - Breaking Down Barriers

Look at that, it seems to be a practice that is inherent in women... to anticipate the emotional state and any possibility of a need in those they care for... why isn't it that way for men?

Men and our pride... you would think that by now, men would have learned that our pride almost always causes us to experience a lost that has an impact that is irreversible. We have been busy following the teachings of other immature, incomplete males that teach us that it's "weak" to show our emotions to our mate. We need to hide or worse yet, pretend that we have no emotional needs. We are unemotional juggernauts, because somewhere along the way, we learned that having emotional strength is weak... it's a woman's trait. Nothing could be further from the truth!

It takes more strength to expose yourself to someone intimately; to reach out to them and invite your partner into the secret knowledge of your goings on. It is an elevated state of maturity that shows the person who is listening that they have a value as the confidant that you trust in when you are troubled. If this is the person who loves you, then is it not the right person to impart that knowledge to?

Yet men think, *"Oh no. I better not tell her.*

Where Is Love? 62

She's gonna know that I feel intimidated and struggle with accessing my courage in certain situations... my God, she's gonna know that I am human and that I'm just a man!"

Mr. Right hurts when she can't accept him; but stop bitching... we do it to them all the time!

Earlier on pg.17 I began to examine how a male can emotionally shut down. This can additionally happen when he is giving his all, yet being taken for granted.

A great man can find himself feeling emasculated, when the woman in his life doesn't prioritize him. This is a very peculiar situation because here you have Mr. Right doing everything in his power to make the relationship work, but he is not feeling appreciated at all. There is no reciprocity and he is unable to establish the connection with her that he feels should be there, if, they love each other. In this scenario, I am not referring to a man that is trying half-heartedly, but a man that genuinely loves his mate and has put his all into making it succeed.

This can be absolutely frustrating, as he starts to think that she does not take him seriously. Or perhaps, she doesn't value him as someone worthy of her attention.

Chapter 2 - Breaking Down Barriers

Unfortunately for him, he continues to grow in loving her more and finds himself trapped because he is doing his best to enlighten her as to the damage she is causing him to experience internally.

Unfortunately, through all of her apologies and speeches of swearing to change, there is never any true move made towards change. So he ends up biding his time, and inserts breaks between them so that he is able to cool off and again later go through the whole process again and yet again. Why continue to accept this treatment, especially when he feels that he is deserving of much better?

In a personal testimonial of my own, I was the above man. I came across a woman that I felt embodied the characteristics of a potential wifey. This woman was intelligent, confident, focused, and beautiful: I just knew I had hit the jackpot... she was the one! [Of course since I am writing about her in here... I was absolutely wrong!]

She appeared to be intelligent, but she only addressed issues that were in her everyday realm of thought, namely her job; outside of that, she was so lost she couldn't allow herself to offer any good conversation.

Where Is Love? 64

Confidence was only there when I was next to her and while I was giving her compliments, so that as she deflated, I inflated her esteem immediately. Time revealed that she was focused as far as presenting a plan, but she never had any drive to complete anything that she ever attempted.

Soon enough her endeavors resembled the nickel and dime money schemes contrived by Ralph Kramden and Fred Flintstone; however, even they both **attempted** the schemes! Her beauty ran as deep as her epidermis, because her thoughts and deeds represented a monster that was so selfish, it still leaves me dumbfounded. I don't say that lightly either.

Once I took her to a concert to celebrate her birthday. At the time, I was going through some things financially, so my pockets were rather slim. I knew that, but I also knew that she had to go out for her birthday, as she was so used to that treatment. There was no way she could accept doing something the following week. So I sacrificed all the money I had and even borrowed extra dollars from my sister.

Now, you would think that with her being aware of this entire situation, she would take it easy on me, yet when the waitress came around for orders, she ordered something outrageously expensive.

Chapter 2 - Breaking Down Barriers   65

My sister being coy, kind of reminded her about money, when she said, "you gonna have enough to feed him too?" Hoping to look good in my sister's eyes, she said, "I'll just get this instead," and ordered some fruit and salad platter.

Some lady that had gotten into the venue early with us, (as my sister sings back up for the artist we had gone to watch), had tagged along as family. She was a nice lady and sat with us and ordered her food when we ordered ours. It was her birthday as well, and she was so excited because my sister had us sitting in VIP, and her original tickets were much further back. My sister was getting ready to take her in the green room to meet the singer. She hurriedly placed an order for exactly what my mate had originally desired to have. She asked us to watch out for her food, so no one would mess with it. We agreed and told her to go have fun, as it was her birthday. Her and my sister took off, but my sister returned in a little while, having set up something special for my lady and the new "family" friend, M.

The food came and M ran over and grabbed some of her fruit and ate some bites from her dinner. My lady friend was eyeing this and seemed to get greener with every bite that M took. M took off into the crowd again.

Where Is Love?

We all continued to eat our orders and when they were done, the waitress had the empty dishes removed. M's food was still there though. My lady, acting as though she were concerned for M, offered to cover up M's meal, but I looked and noticed her actually eating some of it. I couldn't believe it! I was mortified!

I tapped my sister under the table, and my sister said, "Damn, you that hungry... I'll buy you a steak!"

She laughed it off and said, "Well shoot, its getting cold and she ain't eating it!" She even took some more, then covered it up and looked at us like we were wrong for stopping her. My sister looked at me and shrugged, "You sure know how to pick 'em boy!"

Can you imagine that? And this was from a woman that endlessly prided herself as the prototype of what being a lady was. It was utterly disgusting behavior. Yet, for several years I chose to support this woman through all of her selfishness.

When she felt inept as an academic, I applauded her thoughts to support her yearning to display her mental prowess. When she cried nightly over her acne problem and said that she was ugly, I kissed her cheeks and told her she was beautiful. When she decided to start a high-end water company, I put up money to purchase her supplies.

Chapter 2 - Breaking Down Barriers

Or when she tried to come out with her own lipstick, I came up with the logo and name. When she was unemployed and feeling self-pity, I pushed her to go out and interview for jobs.

I thought that maybe since I was older, I owed it to her to be extra patient and be willing to teach some lessons of love.

The lessons never took because she was incapable of dropping her guard and allowing herself to love, yet she was selfish enough to demand the best of me. She never even got close to giving a 50% contribution to the relationship's success. I finally accepted that she was incapable of loving me appropriately.

Here is the gist of this section; I was hurt because I was never a priority of hers. I think that it is of critical importance that I be brutally honest and reveal exactly how badly I felt in the aftermath of my personal Hurricane Senorita.

There is a painful side to the reckless abandonment that these insensitive partners cause to their good mates. Far too often this abandonment goes unnoticed, so I want to share how devastating that pain can be from the inside.

As a man, pride is the major harness of how emotions are either checked or released to run rampant.

Where Is Love? 68

If the pride is diminished via a blow to the ego, hurt is experienced and anger intensifies directly proportionate to the depth of pain.

I found myself hurt beyond repair at that point. I thought I couldn't breathe and that I would never heal. Largely because I had been here before and thought I'd taken every precaution to never allow myself to revisit this sickening state. Regrettably, here I was feeling every bit like a sucker for having relinquished my heart to someone who in no way ever showed me that she deserved my heart, but that's me. Always trying to stay a king and do the noble thing, I offered my heart, as it was meant to teach her that there is an element of risk that comes with wanting to love someone.

As the leader of our relationship, the responsibility fell to me to set the precedent that I would move first, even fearing the worse, to clear the path of all danger for her. I understood and accepted my role.

I was to become her protector and even in this example of risking all, I knew that my actions would reflect my integrity and show my inner strength and courage. I was so busy wanting to please and impress her that I forgot all about my needs.

Chapter 2 - Breaking Down Barriers

I needed to do all of this, but I forgot that I needed to have it appreciated by someone who could truly treasure the effort that I was putting forth. Otherwise, it would all prove to be a waste; now, here we were years later... and it was certainly a waste!

Tears seemed to fall endlessly, and the grand portion of my days was spent reflecting on the minimal good moments that did exist. All the time, my breathing was shallow and I struggled to swallow air properly between the spurts of lamentations.

My head spun uncontrollably, as though I were in a drunken stupor induced by the injections of constant cruelty that I took in steady dosages as the partner of a woman that never considered me her partner. Every song, TV program, DVD; they all reminded me of her, seeing as how I had accumulated so many things to compensate for being alone so much, while with her. I tried to throw things away to rid myself of thinking of her, but then I realized how ignorant that was, as I had purchased those things and would have to replace them.

I lost my ability to eat; loss of hunger and heartbreak seemed to go hand in hand. There seemed to be a strange comfort in suffering.

Yet, what bothered me most about all of this was that I had to endure it, although I never earned it.

I had always treated her as my queen and given her top priority in my eyes. I went through trial after trial with her. I endured all manner of obstacles to prove to her that I was in love with her and that I was in it for the long haul.

My guess is that she never learned how to develop trust in her partner, which caused me to end up suffering constantly as I worked harder and harder to try to breakthrough to her. She believed that she was entitled to the absolute best treatment that a man could deliver, while also believing that no man was close to worthy of her effort.

In the classic case of narcissism... the person finds himself or herself enmeshed in their distorted view of themselves as the object of everyone's attention. They conduct themselves according to the beliefs that they have fabricated, opting to place themselves in the limelight, so to speak. Any and everything must reflect as an image of them being satisfied in as many ways as they can and their happiness is all that counts.

This was definitely the sole characteristic that I can recall being manifested throughout the entirety of the relationship.

Chapter 2 - Breaking Down Barriers   71

As I begged her to learn to reciprocate, the words began to haunt me and gave birth to a resentment of how badly I was being treated.

I think what was most disturbing was that whenever I addressed how badly I felt, she always confessed that she knew she was doing me wrong, but couldn't help herself. This became her consistent defense for why I was being abused by her, but I hated it, because she grew too used to saying it, as though it was the acceptable rationale for my mistreatment. Meanwhile, I kept wondering, why not simply invest the time and energy like I did to learn how to please her mate? I must not be a priority to her!

The particulars of this situation can apply to either sex, but there is a particular reason I went through detailing my mistreatment. I want the men of this world to remember when we are treating our women like that... it can come back to you! You can even find yourself, going through the heartbreaks for no particular reason at all!

Too often, we have very little regard for the after-effects of broken hearts that we have created. If you are a man, you must put in as much effort to repair all damage that you cause, in observance of divine law.

Where Is Love?

Ever notice when men fall in love, how they seem to fall so much harder? The break-up process seems to be far more devastating; consequentially, men initialize most of the murders resulting from break-ups.

We have no real skills in dealing with separation, yet we have no regard for what damage we do. It's time to repair our image as strong men and lead our relationships successfully back to equality between the sexes. We must reestablish the precedence of recognizing our women as *our* equals. We do so by setting our mate as our priority. This is critical to not only the success of our personal relationship, but also the success of other relationships!

So many times others, especially younger others, are watching and they observe our conduct as the basis of their concepts of love. This is a point that needs to be seriously considered, as we end up being the model of what they will come to consider as the basis of their love. We indirectly lay the foundation of what love looks like for them in their very near future. If it is a look we disagree with, we must consider how we helped create it.

Within the context of our personal interaction, I desire to be my mate's all in all and whether you know it or not, she wants you to be her all in all!

Chapter 2 - Breaking Down Barriers

Security is probably the best state that can be established in a relationship because it shows that she is your priority. Real thought was given to understanding who she is, what she wants, and how you plan to provide it for her.

I mentioned in an earlier section that you must realize that you have decided to take on the role that her father once held in her life. This isn't a position that you get yourself into and then sit back wondering how. You chose to be in that role, so you need to do your best in that capacity. But there is a point to be understood here. The motive must be appropriate... your reason for succeeding in the role of her partner needs to reflect your love for her.

I have always held on to an ideology that whenever I ensure her happiness, I actually guarantee my own euphoria, but I never really understood why. Now I know that it is because she is half of me!

It is definitely a move towards my own satisfaction, when I take the necessary steps to bring about her perpetual happiness. After all, my whole reason for being with her is my own pursuit of happiness and search for completion, being fulfilled by my own effort.

Where Is Love? 74

Even so, the greatest strength to be gained is the realization that when you act on the behalf of creating the happiness of someone that you adore, selflessly... you experience a growth in your character. This assists you in following that path easier and causes you to shine more with each subsequent act.

Women fantasize – everybody likes me; Men ponder – does she like me...

Almost intrinsically, women are born with an innate need to be accepted. This usually translates into one perpetual statement... that everybody likes, and there fore accepts her. This belief is often the major contributor to her deception in her various love relationships. It inspires a grand amount of her actions just as well. Let me start at the beginning.

A little girl, Megan, is born into a single parent family, which her father, Mason has never been a part of. Little Megan has always heard that her father was such a ladies' man: to the point that he seemed to have been celebrated for his womanizing ways.

All the grown-up women seemed to clamor around adoringly whenever Mason came through town. They would linger about swooning from the acts and intentions of this Urban Celebrity.

Chapter 2 - Breaking Down Barriers

They were all hoping that for just an instant in time, he would select them; they would be the one!

Dotty was considered the cutest girl in town and every male wanted her, but knew that it was impossible to have her, as she had been raised in a strict, Christian home to be a "good" girl. The usual fast-talking, slick-acting boys of her hometown, stared hungrily as starved country dogs in a butcher's freezer, when they saw her.

On one of his many visits to town, Mason happened to stumble into a chance encounter with Dotty. The usual cavalier gallivanting and braggadocio that served as the premier weapons of his conquests, would certainly lay the foundation for his undoing on this specific day. It is said that to the victor go the spoils, but by the time Dotty would send Mason off... he would meet himself for the first time!

Dotty worked in Evan's diner, where she had become quite the rave for her ability to make everyone feel special and spoil them with her attention to customer service. As Mason entered the diner, he spied Dotty at work. He had previously intended to return to this diner for the specific purpose of conquering Dotty.

This conquest would definitely cost him all of his chauvinistic ways and ultimately mature him into being a real man; for once, if he wanted the woman, he would have to invest his heart.

Being his usual arrogant self, he approached her in his most audacious alpha pounce, fully expecting from her no more than the normal public resistance for the sake of not being viewed as a town whore.

"Hello Mason. How are you today?" "Hey doll." "Know what you want?" "Do I? I came here today, specifically to fulfill my taste for it."

"Well, let's have it... what will it be?" "One hot dog bun and... hmmm, what goes best on a dog Dotty?" "I dunno. I guess... well I like sauerkraut." "Then that's what you'll, er... I mean I'll have."

Dotty left and went and got what Mason had ordered wondering the whole time, what type of nonsense he was up to. She decided to go and prepare the bread herself. In a few minutes she was headed back towards the table where Mason had repositioned himself. She gave him his order. *"Ok. Here ya go and I won't ask."* Mason took the plate and sat it down.

He then reached under the table and freed himself. He grabbed the hot dog bun and placed himself within it.

Chapter 2 - Breaking Down Barriers

Then he spread the sauerkraut to help disguise his deed a bit better. Dotty walked by just as he had positioned the plate just right. *"What the hell are you up to Mason?"* *"I just thought, no one ever serves you, so I figured I would take the time to do so. Here. I know you'll love it!"* Dotty feigned, allowing time to lapse just enough. Mason's face started to show signs of discomfort, while Dotty condescendingly began to explain. *"See, I knew you were up to something, so I prepared that bun extra-special for you."* *"Argh... oh shit... my dick's on fire..."* He took off screaming, plowing down everything between himself and the bathroom.

When he returned, he stood there with his pants unzipped and himself wet and exposed. Dotty said, *"Hots for the hottie."* Mason hung his head low in shame as he confessed, *"Ok, I definitely deserved that. I was just trying to get your attention."*

Dotty felt no sympathy for him. Mason may have been seeking sympathy, but he was being chastened. In an unrelenting style of admonishment she stated, *"Well you don't have to be a jerk to do so. I am not the rest of your town groupies."* Once Mason reined his hormones and machismo in, he was a decent guy.

Where Is Love? 78

Without question he was easy on the eyes and she had secretly wanted him, but was trying to have him address her properly. This was in hopes that he would act as a gentleman versus being the brute he so often put on display. Of course, Mason being the player that he was, he played the role of a gentleman to a tee, until he got what he wanted.

Some months later, Dotty was pregnant and as much as she had hoped that Mason had changed, the more she learned that he was an even worse womanizer. Now a disillusioned Dotty was left to raise her daughter Meagan all on her own.

In that household, Meagan could recall all too often her mom referring to her dad as "that son of a bitch."

Mason is the prototype of far too many males, that have not learned to respect women; but, the truth is that they do not respect themselves. They have no desire to do anything other than conquer a woman. Not in a search for her quality, these males seek only a female with a pretty face and an appeasing body; a willing figure, with a seductive smile and a non-resistant embrace. Remember too many of these young men are still seeking a girl and they fear engaging in any exchange with a **woman**.

Chapter 2 - Breaking Down Barriers

So these guys spend their time mastering every practical understanding of girls: their desires, their motives, and how best to manipulate them. Soon enough, they discover that females that haven't grown up with their fathers are usually the easiest targets for sexual conquests.

Sadly, these girls tend to search for a replacement for that fatherly love and end up suffering while looking in all the wrong places when they endure the loss of their fathers. Additionally, they end up engaging in all sorts of acts in an effort to be accepted and ultimately loved.

They surmise that in this manner they can ultimately capture that which has escaped them for a lifetime... the number one spot in a male's eyes.

Love is an objective that each female is pursuing, but that they really don't understand to well. This is weird because in the usual stages of development, females tend to have such a strong grasp on tapping into their emotions, although they may not have mastered a complete understanding. As daddy's love and acceptance of her will be her first opportunity to be subjected to being scrutinized, the father's role is intensely intricate in their daughter's development.

Where Is Love?

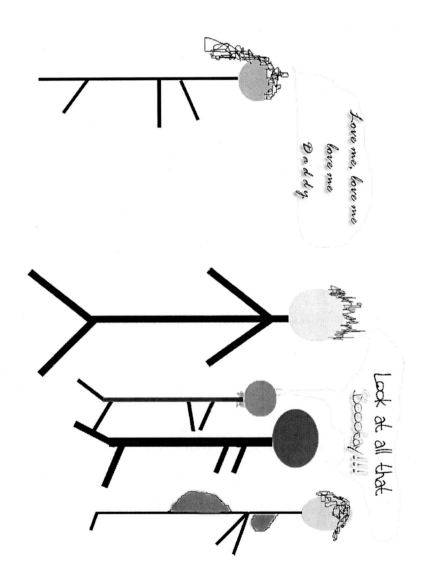

Chapter 2 - Breaking Down Barriers

Unfortunately this is so often overlooked. [For more on this topic, read my book, *I Believe.*]

The women who remain stuck in this cycle are doomed to repeat their actions until they encounter a man that truly has an understanding of his influence on this phenomenon within her. He must be a man that is beyond the low self-esteem state himself, as it seems that the poor interaction between a parent and a child, especially of the opposing sex, creates a deficit in self-esteem in all children.

Children are constantly evolving into the adults they are to become; they conceptualize their importance and sense of worth from their inner circle, the nuclear family. When they receive the proper attention, this is interpreted as their acceptance and they build high self-esteem and see themselves as not just worthy of all that is good, but as a part of the greater society... they belong. Isn't that the purpose of seeking a relationship in the first place... to find someone that you can belong to, where you will be viewed as a priority and loved without conditions?

In so many ways, this is an adult's attempt at recreating the security of the relationship they cherished with their parent, as a child.

Where Is Love?   82

This is how we are validated and provided with an external assessment of our value... we still need that instant gratification as a human being. Age doesn't change that need; it generates a requirement for a new methodology of how we obtain that instant gratification as adults.

I guess it shouldn't be such a surprise that as adults, we still require these acts of affection that will guarantee our satisfaction. This is a carnal desire inside of man: a fundamental yearning to reconnect to our appropriate chronological position. To understand this desire, it is critical to have an understanding of the spiritual side of being human. It is even more important to understand how traumatic experiences can stunt the growth of a person.

Whenever a human being encounters something traumatic, (a parent abandoning them, a first love cheating on them, their home burning down during their childhood, etc.), the spirit of that person pauses its growth and does not continue to grow anymore. That spirit will not begin to grow again until the trauma that started the stunted growth, has been healed.

Chapter 2 - Breaking Down Barriers

Now why is this important; because so often I hear complaints from different partners in couples that they wish that their mate would grow up or that their mate is so childish and immature. In fact, that very complaint is much more accurate than they even realize.

By knowing their mate's traumatic experience, they may be able to assist them in healing and therefore growing beyond that incident. Sometimes the person hasn't healed from an experience because they didn't have the support or perhaps they haven't been able to recognize the effects of that trauma on their life as a whole. It is during this time though that people develop low self-esteem and lack self-confidence and begin to seek external approval. This can lead a person towards very destructive behavior when they aren't strong enough to see their own value.

Having a strong, supportive partner provides them with a set of objective eyes that are probing them and looking for improvements that will allow them to grow and be a better person. This person also provides a secondary voice that can prompt them to behave in ways that are positive, rather than simply acting on impulse.

Where Is Love?

In summary, the need of being accepted exists in both sexes and usually stems from loss of a parent's approval and attention during the developmental stages. Coupled with a traumatic incident, the spirit of a youth can become stunted and cause the person to not grow spiritually. When there is no spiritual growth, negative actions most certainly will result and the morality of this individual will become questionable. This occurs with or without the individual acknowledging it, and can become a cycle of torment. In this state the self-esteem is depleted and only having objective support or honing the positive energy of one's spirit can break this cycle and finally allow the individual to grow again spiritually. So here, love from a trusted partner and love of one's self, provide the healing needed to break the cycled behavior of low self-esteem.

You Fucking bastards... the Married and Womanizing!

I don't know what it is, but for as long as I can remember, married guys have always had to have the extra girl on the side. When you consider something simple like an evening at the gentleman's club, the place is usually loaded with married guys who are all drowning their woes in drinks and lamentations of being married.

Chapter 2 - Breaking Down Barriers

While these married men are telling the worse stories about being married, what they are really doing is causing all the unmarried guys to look at marriage as something that they definitely don't want to have any part of ... E V E R!

These guys hog up the best of the women to themselves, while making the single guys hate the idea of perpetual commitment. Now how's that as a plan for ensuring and protecting one's dibs on a resource that you don't want to share? Usually I am cautious about not being a hater to any man's success with women, but I tend to be one of those guys that run into these "once upon a time were great" women, AFTER they have been burned by these misogynists. I absolutely hate that because I end up being punished for a practice that I don't even understand myself.

So Do I Sound Spiteful?

HELL yeah... you guys tend to get the best selection of women; those that love dedicating themselves to their men. There's a peculiar aspect to attraction that whenever a person is attached to someone else they tend to look outstandingly more attractive.

Where Is Love?

There is something special about going after someone that is already attached; they have value. Their unavailability creates an air of attractiveness that encompasses them; unfortunately, even if the seeker has no idea that this object of their affection is in another relationship, they still seem so desirable. Let me be clear about one thing though.

All of you women who find yourselves in those failed relationships... you deserve all the hell that comes with them.

I say that because you will always pass us great guys by, opting in exchange to give your good attention to these fools who can in no way appreciate the beauty of who you are! I apologize for being hard on you, but if I plan on giving all my love to a woman, I owe it to myself to do a bit of research... [Remember pg.5] and make sure that the path is clear.

Too often we are so ready to be swept up and swooned and are willing to ignore inquiring into the obvious, simply because we just want to feel good with that person. We do this not even caring about how much damage can be incurred by our own souls.

Loneliness is a mother fucker... I know I haven't used foul language anywhere else in this book, but there is no other point where it has been as appropriate.

Getting back to the topic... it is so unfortunate that we aren't all of a like mind in relationships. There are the givers and the takers. The givers tend to overcompensate and are willing to bend over backwards to make a love connect work, although it almost always will fail. There is an attraction to being needed that the giver can't seem to ignore. To their chagrin, the givers can not distinguish which prospect will genuinely appreciate their effort, versus creating an endless black hole of selfishness, wherein that very same giver will be slowly siphoned until ultimately being sucked to death of their all.

Now speaking from the perspective of a classic giver type, I have gone over it again and again and still can not figure out what it is that so often causes givers to be most attracted to those who will most abuse them. The best I could come up with is that somewhere deep within our subconscious we really think that we don't deserve the best and therefore constantly subject ourselves to the same punishment over and over.

I haven't been able to clearly determine whether this is the result of a lifetime of insults that we have sustained and witnessed that shape that idea in our minds, but I have noticed that most givers do share that particular characteristic.

It seems like most givers sustain an early love deficit from someone significant [usually a parent], who should have provided them with critical developmental love, and since they never received that love, they equate it to them not deserving it. This begins the pattern of overcompensating or rather making up for not being love-worthy. As crazy as that seems, it reappears in case study after case study of the "giver" role.

An interesting point is that the taker usually comes from an identical background of circumstances, but chooses the reactive path of trying to fulfill their love deficit, where the giver chooses the proactive path. The giver believes they don't deserve love, while the takers believe the world owes it to them. Perhaps the submissiveness of the giver is naturally being exploited by the dominance of the taker and this is simply a biological trait of each type.

Chapter 2 - Breaking Down Barriers

Too often, the impact of these roles are passed over and often not even discussed. Maybe that is how the married men with women on the side and womanizers in general are able to prosper at their mischief. Perhaps that is the real issue to be discussed... this disparity of equality between the givers and takers. Ever notice how the rule of opposites seems to always apply; unfortunately, it applies in a negative aspect far more than in a positive capacity.

As I began to disclose men problems on pg.31, another element under consideration emerged which might further explain why married men tend to carry on their womanizing ways. Their actions allow them to hide their deficits... especially the inability to communicate effectively.

A married man may find himself unable to voice his opinion adequately at home with his wife, who is strong and an evolved version of his mother. To compensate for all the times that she controls the dialogue, he refrains from talking with his side woman, which is usually a grand aspect of the clandestine affair. Neither side is privy to wanting to discuss too much as being secretive is the main component in having a "friend with benefits" situation.

Where Is Love?   90

A point that eludes these men, is that the women involved may still be holding the upper hand as they elect this course of action to minimize their leading role in the unbalanced relationships that they usually are in. Too many of them are always looked to for their strength in these relationships and they seek to temporarily be seen as a demure, beautiful woman. This situation caters to their desire to be admired in a superficial manner. This isn't about someone being their true complement or someone that they confide in, but rather the source of the physical appreciation that a woman needs to experience to continue feeling pretty.

Probing further into these deficits of married men, we come to a horrific, yet commonly possessed deficit among them. That being, the tendency to marry based on external pressures... from maternal urging to premarital pregnancy to the need to preserve one's reputation amongst the church congregation. I believe that many of these men believe that they are doing something noble, but a true king knows his throne and would never do anything that jeopardizes his ability to sit upon that throne, uninterrupted.

Chapter 2 - Breaking Down Barriers

I would like to take a moment and examine each of these particular situations to attempt to provide the rationale for why succumbing to these are not appropriate courses of action.

Let's begin with the man that marries because his mom is coercing him into getting tied down, because she says she wants him to have a family. Does she want him to have a family... yes, she may actually want some grand children and he is going to comply. This is, of course, a bad choice because in its initial inception you have a man making a potential lifelong commitment even though he had no desire to commit himself to any woman in that manner yet. He can't act out against his mother, so his wife will be the permanent recipient of all of his strife for having been pushed into doing what he didn't want to. As time passes, his children will incur this same fate, either direct or indirect and they will learn from his actions to devalue their mother. Ultimately, the children will lack respect for women and view them as weak; the female children will suffer low self-esteem because they will internalize this way of life as their eventual destiny.

Next, there is the submission to pressure from the impending pregnancy of the woman in his life because they have indulged in a sexual situation and she has become pregnant prior to getting married.

This is probably one of the weakest of these situations because it honestly suggests that he is covering his tracks under pressure from being ostracized from his peers simply based on tradition and norms. Again, the fruit of this union will most likely become subject to the effects of the father's inner turmoil as his mind seeks to relieve itself of the angst of not being allowed to make the choices that he wanted to make, especially if he should end up having a child that he isn't particularly close to or fond of.

Oh yes, every parent won't like their children simply because they are theirs. Let's not even play the game and pretend that this isn't so. Now consider with that as the setting in a home, how far down the path of dysfunction will this particular family head?

Finally, there is the man that married because of his promise to God to be a good Christian. For whatever reason, many Christians believe that it's better for them to jump head first into the worse possible union rather than to simply walk away.

Chapter 2 - Breaking Down Barriers

The controlling grip of some congregations and the pastor in charge can coerce a man into choosing a marriage that he cannot escape unless they sanction the end of that marriage.

In such a situation, we find a man that feels emasculated and utterly powerless over an aspect of his adult life that easily most affects his journey through adulthood. From this point forward he will doubt his ability to make his own choices. Having shorted himself in the exchange of preserving his image versus being true to his ideas and intentions, he now will lose his stability and balance in life. The once powerful gait in his walk will become replaced with the slouching shoulders and a lowered head. Should he have any male children, they may adopt this defeated attitude as well and his daughters will never respect him as a strong man and will learn to adopt a concept of emasculating men.

It is mandatory that in a marriage that produces offspring, the children MUST see strong, healthy, positive examples of who they are to grow up to be. Men in these situations will most likely be unable to provide that example and eventually the guilt of being an incomplete man will manifest itself in their infidelity.

Where Is Love? 94

The sad part is that in each and every one of these situations, the man had a choice to select a course of action that he really wanted to have occur, but the truest deficit is his weakness for not being able to commit to his own self. Man is commanded to lead and he can't possibly do that when he sacrifices his will to the external force of what outside pressures dictate to him as the correct path to take. He further hurts himself by destroying the best in his offspring by providing an insubstantial role to be modeled. Recall the attributes of a man [pg.50], and that these choices contradict those attributes sharply.

Chapter 3 – Applying What U Learned

I wish that the "me" of 17 had the knowledge of the "me " of now... man I'd be awesome! -Prose

Ok, no more games... keeping it real, how about keeping it honest?

"I keep it real!" How often have you heard that statement? You know what? I hate that statement. Anyone that is true to those words doesn't need to convince you of their honesty by yelling it out. I see it as the copout statement for those looking for validation from a popular consensus of observers that don't probe deeply enough to discern the integrity of anyone. It is a twisted norm of sorts, amongst those with deficits, to keep the light of inquisition from digging deeply into who they are and what they are about.

There is another dual-sided criterion that needs to be considered when thinking about honesty in a relationship; a revealing partner can only be as honest as their receiving partner is prepared to accept. Although revealing partners have a responsibility to speak in earnest to their mates, how much can they share if their partner is unwilling to hear the truth? They simply can't be honest all the time.

Where Is Love?

This is to maintain a sense of nobility, by opting to protect their partner from the truth, but it can also be out of a sense of desperation because their mate will come into the knowledge of how lowdown they truly are as a person.

Now we all know that honesty is necessary in a relationship, but I wonder whether you all understand why. I know that I didn't have any idea why for the longest time. What's more important is that not until I learned why, was I able to fully respect and cherish having an honest bond between us, which in turn fueled my desire to be more open with my mate. This made open communication more appealing and something to value, as we sought to grow closer. What once seemed of no real consequence to us now had become an essential building block upon which we could rest the foundation of our love.

Please pay attention, especially those of you who think little white lies aren't anything really big to complain about.

When you lie to your mate, you take away their ability to utilize their free will and their ability to choose how they want to deal with the situation.

Chapter 3 – Applying What U Learned

You show your mate that you have absolutely no respect for their ability to assess the situation and address it appropriately. This is critical seeing as how you have already damaged your partner's trust, now you are further adding insult to injury by indirectly controlling them. Yes, I said controlling them! Well you are, seeing as how you are manipulating the situation to go in your favor without allowing that person to select any option of their own volition to bring about redemption.

You continue to lie further by trying to pretend that you have done this for their benefit, but it is actually your selfishness on major display. You have no real concern for the pain you have caused; you simply want the easiest way out of what you have done. The foundation that was being built for your love is now encountering major erosion.

Far too many people make the mistake of underestimating how devastating a blow is actually dealt when they tell those little white lies. If you allow yourself to recall that this person is the love of your life, you will also recall that being honest will bring you closer to each other. Even the little white lie is too much of a detriment and can tear you and your partner apart. You may find that your partner can never recover from the incident!

See... there is nothing little about this action at all.

Why place your ultimate happiness in jeopardy over something so miniscule?

I know it may seem like an enormous task to be responsible for your interactions with your mate, but that couldn't be further from the truth, because this person is half of you.

Let me enlighten you... all you have to do is be completely honest... just once! This will lay the foundation for you to follow up with more honesty and transition you into being able to handle the stress of delivering sensitive information without feeling pressured to be dishonest. This frees you to be all out open with your partner and creates the gateway to a state of lifetime happiness. You will have mastered one of the components of creating perpetual happiness between your mate and yourself.

This is a gift... by far it's nothing to sneeze at, as most people may never come to know the beauty of this sense of comfort in their relationship. You have honestly unlocked the door to one of the secrets to keeping your relationship healthy and at its best.

Chapter 3 – Applying What U Learned   99

One small step for a man... **one** gigantic leap
forward for his relationship!

This is truly the final frontier for most human beings; love itself is the state we most want to be in, yet we have the hardest time learning how to get there. The culmination of all the things I have spoken of to this point can collectively provide one with techniques to gain a solid understanding of love, what it means and how to secure it. This is why I felt the need to write this book.

I honestly believed that from all the problems I saw, experienced and heard of, I had come up with practical solutions to enable people of both sexes and all races to be able to embrace each other in a loving capacity. One might wonder why I place the topic of honesty so far back into the book, but I felt the other layers of defense had to be stripped away, as most of us have developed hardened ways of presenting our hearts to our partners.

I am here to tell you that the love of a lifetime that you want can be secured and maintained forever.

Where Is Love? 100

Does it require some significant effort on your behalf... of course, but in this life, anything that will ultimately benefit you, requires you to put your best foot forth.

Love don't hurt you (the proof) 1 Cor. 13:4-8

Have you ever found yourself on the low end of self-esteem, wondering whether anyone loves you? Have you ever even considered whether there is a true definition of what love is? Well, having sustained some pretty hard knocks against my heart, I often found myself in this predicament and sought to find some solace in the way of an incontestable explanation of love. In earnest, this was actually an immeasurable need-to know-item that I had been craving my whole life! This longtime need worked on my heart like the erosion of Atlantic Ocean's coastline.

Yes, love is that special common meeting place of two hearts intertwined for the sole purpose of perpetuating each other's happiness, but it goes beyond just the secular realm... it involves more than just the body. The spirit ultimately must be in harmony with the intentions of the heart and additionally in sync with the potential partner. So as hard as I looked, I failed to find anything of consequence that truly addressed the nascent void within me.

Chapter 3 – Applying What U Learned

Accompanying this burgeoning emptiness, was an increasing sense of worthlessness that speedily diminished my value of self; I began to feel as though I did not deserve love and that was why it seemed to consistently escape me.

Where is love... please tell me where?
What the F is love?
Does anyone know?

As I stated, I had an innate need to clarify what exactly love is, especially as I began to accept that I had never experienced it. My mother abandoned me as a youth, so on a developmental love level... I had nothing to even remotely begin to build on or attach my thoughts to as an example of what love should look like.

Among my peers, the subject was almost taboo as anyone probing would be ridiculed and ultimately ostracized. But why? Was love really that intense of a topic, that even though we all needed it and craved it, it would be better to wonder alone lost seeking its meaning? My simple adolescent question was beginning to take on all the characteristics of an adult quest towards self-revelation.

Where Is Love? 102

During my adolescent years, my auntie set an example for me by always referring to the Bible when things became too much to bear. As this appeared to be one of those times, I took time and began to research the topic of love. I figured this was the most appropriate place to gain an understanding of love... where the greatest love story of all time took place. There is something about a serious search that elevates your ability to digest content in a more fulfilling way than the normal face value acceptance of a basic premise. I was searching and searching and just as I thought it was turning into an act of futility... the truth revealed itself.

I can't begin to tell you how great it felt to finally encounter something tangible that put in place exactly what I so desperately needed to define. I was lacking meaning and here it was in bold print. I had found the answer to the secret to my happiness and ultimately the happiness of everyone who desires to live a fulfilling life with their rightful companion.

This whole book has been geared at assisting you, the reader in hopefully obtaining the ability to discern the deficits within your relationship that have plagued it.

Chapter 3 – Applying What U Learned

Furthermore, it has been filled with tips to provide you with the insight to determine the root cause of those deficits and design a practical solution to be applied to correct these deficiencies. After this stage, you next learn how to engage in the harmonious exchange of commitment and fulfillment. Finally... you will execute these techniques to guarantee a perpetual state of bliss amongst partners and spouses that will become visually noticeable and serve as the model of love to all that observe.

Of all the information I have provided in this book, this is the most significant jewel of them all, as it truthfully answers the question of what love is and how to know when you are being loved genuinely. I am sure that each and every one of you has at some point questioned the validity of the love of someone that you wanted to believe in with all your heart. So for every one of you, here is the only definition you will ever need... 1 Corinthians 13:4-8.

Probably the first thing to understand in this verse is the key word *charity*. This word is synonymous with Christian love, Agape and suggests a sense of benevolence towards those in need.

Where Is Love?   104

This is a love modeled after the concept of the savior of the world: the one person who sacrifices himself for the survival of us all, symbolically showing that sacrifice is at the center of loving others. I wanted to explain this before starting the verse; because this establishes the appropriate mindset that one needs to be in when professing one's love. Your love is always being presented in order to address someone's need.

I am going to write out the verse first in its completion to allow you to gauge the definition in its entirety.

1 Corinthians 13: 4] *Charity suffereth long, and is kind; charity envieth not: vaunteth not itself, is not puffed up. 5] Doth not behave itself unseemly, seeketh not her own, is not easily provoked, thinketh no evil: 6] Rejoiceth not in iniquity, but rejoiceth in the truth: 7] Beareth all things, believeth all things, hopeth all things, endureth all things. 8] Charity never faileth:*

Please take a minute and reread this again... slowly; I need this to really settle in because there is quite a lot of information to consider and take in here. *All* of these attributes collectively are love! Not most, not some, but all of them *together* make up love. This is forever going to become the basis and set the precedence for what you will accept as love from now on.

Chapter 3 – Applying What U Learned

Notice that I have not said "real" love or "true" love, and the reason why is because love is love. It shouldn't need to be authenticated or have its value assigned, because it is genuine and does have significance on its own.

1 Corinthians 13: 4] *Charity suffereth long, and is kind; charity envieth not; vaunteth not itself, is not puffed up.* Someone who loves you is able to put up with all obstacles, is patient and treats you good; isn't jealous; They do not boast or brag, isn't one that makes themselves look like more than they are, they don't send you a representative, they are their genuine self.

1 Corinthians 13: 5] *Doth not behave itself unseemly, seeketh not her own, is not easily provoked, thinketh no evil;* A person who loves you does not act in ways that cause you to feel embarrassed or uncomfortable, they understand that their actions are a reflection of you, they put you first and have made you their priority, they act with the best intentions for your betterment, they don't have a hidden agenda and aren't scheming to take advantage of you, they don't bring up things from the past, such as favors they have done and then throw them up in your face. They understand that favors are just that and should be done because they can assist you when in need; after all they're your partner.

Where Is Love? 106

Recall the earlier mindset, your love is always being presented in order to assist someone who has a need. They don't easily get mad with you, they understand tolerance and the fact that you are an individual and have a perspective that isn't quite the same as their own. They want to respect you.

The person that loves you cannot look at you and think the worse of you; with regards to you, they are a constant optimist. They see the good in you, even when no one else does. They don't waste time constantly reminding you of the misdeeds that you may have engaged in during the past and forever hold it against you; the person that loves you is your personal cheerleader!

1 Corinthians 13: 6] *Rejoiceth not in iniquity, but rejoiceth in the truth:* A person that loves you takes no pleasure in you or themselves doing wrong, they like when things are done in an orderly manner and with a righteous intent; they celebrate your integrity and by doing so, assist you in perpetuating the cycle of being your best self all the time. As humans, we tend to find it easier to do things in more of a negative manner. It requires true courage to fight through selfish laziness and push forward & decide to be our best selves.

Chapter 3 – Applying What U Learned

The support of the partner can be a source for reiteration of why being the best self is beneficial to the union.

1 Corinthians 13: 7] *Beareth all things, believeth all things, hopeth all things, endureth all things.* A person that loves you acts as a partner and assists you in bringing things to fruition in your relationship, they are the spark plug for progress even when you don't have the energy or desire to do what's best for yourself.

They don't just push you to do things, they set an example by going ahead and putting things in motion first, they understand the need to risk themselves by acting first, they believe that together you can accomplish anything and be successful. The person that loves you looks forward to positive things occurring, and loves you in spite of your faults.

1 Corinthians 13: 8] *Charity never faileth;* When a person loves you they will always be there for you. They make it their business to prioritize you and see your happiness as their responsibility. They feel obligated to make sure that you know that they have your back in everything that matters to you.

Where Is Love?   108

Love is never an act of non-reciprocity... it cannot come back without achieving its intentions and as painful as the truth may be, if it returns void, *it isn't love!*

Now, you may not be religious, but if you just really let yourself be open to this new concept, it has to rejuvenate your heart. How beautiful the whole definition is, that it encompassed in such short text, the holistic experience of all that one endures in the pursuit of love. Test it for yourself, heck I did!

For a whole week after I learned this verse, I sat and thought of every messed up scenario that had EVER happened to me in all of my relationships. Then I applied the verse to that situation and found that time after time, I would have been comforted had the person involved utilized all of the love definition.

Now, I don't wanna go getting holier than thou either, because I sure have made my share of goofs in relationships. I fervently believe that a man will never become a great lover until he suffers loss, because that is the only way men seem to learn and evolve.

Simply coming into the knowing of what's appropriate won't assure that a man applies that knowledge for his betterment. But let that same man, lose the love of their life, and he softens into clay.

Chapter 3 – Applying What U Learned

Once this occurs, he is able to be molded and finds himself morphing into a greater version of himself. He becomes a product of the latest upgrade for the newest addition to manhood.

Where Is Love?

Picking & Timing...

In the opening chapter to this book, I shared one of my most prominent philosophical views for how deficits accrue in relationships. As I have begun to do various readings across the country, suggestions have poured in and one of particular interest centered around my "picking" theory. I was continuously asked, "What if we both pick each other, will that alone guarantee that our relationship will work out?" Of course I had to be frank with them and admit that it wouldn't, but that led me to thinking deeper about the process and how it could be improved to bring about a higher percentage of success. What I came up with ultimately was that selection has a secondary assistive factor that must be in sync with it, and that is timing.

Both parties can select each other, but if they do it at the wrong time, there will not be any chance for true success. Both parties have to be available; by that I mean, absolutely open to the impending state of commitment that a loving relationship entails. People often decide that they like someone and want to be with that person, but their life may be in turmoil at that point. They are not truly available... not by a long shot!

Chapter 3 – Applying What U Learned   111

I remember when I was younger, I approached this girl that I liked, Tamika, and asked her to be my girlfriend and she said, "I got to think about it for a little while." This of course, was killing me because patience was the last thing I had left to spare when I had just allowed this girl to see me at my most vulnerable. Didn't she realize how nerve-wracking it was to simply out of the blue walk up to the prettiest girl in school, and with all my flaws and imperfections, request the privilege of being her one and only? Especially when I was doing so without any hints or hook-ups; no one had suggested that she liked me and she certainly hadn't told me anything that made me feel as though she felt towards me, how I did towards her.

Well anyhow, the point here was that she requested this "time" to figure it out. It freaked me out because I never knew what she had to figure out. In my mind, either you liked me or not! The not knowing was so tumultuous that I couldn't sleep the first night of my wait. The next day, I wanted so badly to run to Tamika and ask her whether she had made a decision, but I knew it would make me seem desperate, so I played cool and decided against it.

Where Is Love? 112

Another day passed, and I was every bit as antsy again, but I gave in to my curiosity and inquired only to be engulfed by her perennial statement of independence... *"Don't rush me... I'm a lady."* I was like, *"Hungh... what the heck does that mean? I think she's trying to play me out."*

My self-esteem ebbed and I could see my ultimate rejection, just beyond the next horizon. Day four rolled in with the ferocity of ten starving lions and I once again had to check my irrepressible impulse to inquire about my status. Here I was a wreck and she was parading around just as cool and calm as ever, as though the whole situation had barely raised her eyebrow.

On the fifth day she ran up to me in the hallway, but my mind was so preoccupied I hadn't even noticed that she had come seeking me, or that she was smiling from ear to ear, or that she had something handwritten in her hand and was motioning for me to take it. I instead, lost my cool and blew my top. I began to yell that she was cold and that it sucked that I liked her so much but she didn't even care what I felt. Then I did the ultimate booboo... one that still plagues me to this day.

Chapter 3 – Applying What U Learned

I rescinded my request to be her boyfriend, and in that exact moment of my premature declaration of saving face, I realized just how much I had not noticed. All that I hadn't seen became painfully clear.

As she cried, her left hand began to release the crumpled love note that revealed just how she had always liked me and was so happy that I was brave enough to come to her as I had; the very same note that had her address and phone number in it for me. The same letter that answered my question with an emphatic "yes, I always wanted to be your girlfriend."

Wow, I am sitting here just reliving the whole ordeal and the tears still fight to climb out the corners of my optical openings as tenaciously as a dog seeking exit from its kennel. Dayum, 5 days... was that so much time? It obviously was critical to our happiness or ultimate heartbreak, but I had missed the point.

Time... if I had given her that time, then what? So did I know what that time represented? No. Regardless, I should have respected Tamika's need to exercise her use of that time though, because she was using it for the proposed eventual state of both of our interests. See, clearly, everything was a go on both sides in that memory.

Where Is Love?

I wanted her and she wanted me as well, but timing clearly was the deciding factor that broke this camel's back. What may be more of an epiphany here is the idea that timing may actually be a matter of maturing and learning to respect each other's modus operandi and mental proclivity. I have replayed that memory in my head a million times and on every run through, I pause and want to kick myself in the butt because I realize that I had no respect for her individuality. I missed the essence of what would have been required of me to be a great partner in the relationship. I was immature and inexperience played right into the whole demise of our rapport.

Timing... mine was definitely off! Here I am telling this young lady that essentially I wanted to cherish and love her, but I couldn't appreciate her moving in her own way... that is a problem that too many of us still suffer from.

Fortunate for me, I *suffered through loss early,* and learned the lesson as a youth. Recall when I said that males tend to only be able to learn the real lessons of love through loss. Appreciation comes when we are able to recognize the value of whatever, or rather whoever we have lost the opportunity to be with.

Chapter 3 – Applying What U Learned

So I took that loss and became the wiser for it, but far too many men have not learned to respect the individuality of the one that they are pursuing. And what does that say about you... it shows that you are impatient, obviously, but it more so illustrates someone that needs to control the entire situation.

You do not have trust in the person to decide in favor of you without your direct influence. In essence, you are not displaying the qualities of love; you actually are taking on the look of the type of man that acts unruly in his relationship. Furthermore, you have no true concept of what it means to value yourself and because you don't find yourself to be of value, you expect that everyone else will see you the same way.

Ironically, I had a chance to ask several younger females, what exactly they were making the young requestor wait for and they all said that they needed to see if this person was a good fit. Did he deserve to be with her, because her friends would certainly be full of criticism? Did he treat her right, because her parents would certainly have commentary? Did he respect her, because her heart would certainly have intuition? So timing is more or less an assessment of value, which means that selection must be accompanied with a concept of value and availability.

Where Is Love?   116

Of similar uncanny coincidence, when I inquired about the same topic from older, adult women, they reported similar thoughts. Time was being utilized as a period of self-value assessment.

OOOoooh, you sooo nasty... yeah right. Grow Up!

The end of this project is nearing and I have certainly relished the whole experience of creating this book, but I am really going to enjoy writing this chapter. I have wanted to address the issue of sexual interaction being something "nasty" for my entire life. This is definitely a personal sore spot for me and I am going to be brave and allow you all to share in the knowledge of one of my greatest woes.

Being that I am of African American decent, I have had the opportunity to observe specific trends amongst this community in depth. Although I have seen similarities in other cultures, I believe that there is a specific attitude towards sex that exists in the Diaspora, wherein older adults utilize a scare tactic of creating a phobia of anything sexual, being perceived as something of disgust. This is done as an easy solution to honestly addressing the complex subject of sex with their children, which a great many parents find nerve-wracking.

Chapter 3 – Applying What U Learned

Rather than sit the youth down and be honest, they opt to say things like, "If you give a girl a hickie, she'll lose her virginity." Or another rather stupid, but renowned statement of this type is, "Girls with hickies on them are whores!" Just stop and think about those two statements. The inanity of saying such outright bias statements to the minds of youths would certainly create inhibitions in those youth or give a person at their most vulnerable, volatile state, a serious complex.

This was exactly what happened to me as a youth. My biological, as I refer to her, was always full of her own personal fears with regards to being sexually responsible and having been the product of years of the scare tactic sex education technique, she never developed the courage to seek an explanation of sexual interaction for herself and ultimately passed this foolishness on to me.

As a youth, I was rather popular, so I guess that gave her the premise to begin the poisoning technique on me. It began by her telling me the first statements I mentioned about hickies and gradually became more heinous. "If a girl lets you sleep with her, she is a whore! Sex is a nasty and disgusting thing! You should not be doing it. If you do, I'll know you were doing the devil's work."

Where Is Love?   118

All of these different statements, along with her misinterpretations of the Bible, began to slowly build a complex within me over time. I did not know this was happening yet, because in earnest, I wasn't really interested in sex yet, but her fears were at an all time high.

What she failed to realize was that all of her rhetoric was actually making me more curious to engage in sex and more suspicious of Christianity. See, I have always been one to put a topic to test. There was no way I was going to accept sex as being the heinous act that she spoke of, or the devil's way of stealing your soul. I mean Sis. Holy of Holies must've forgotten that she had indulged in it quite a few times to manufacture my later siblings and myself, but I hadn't! Supposedly my father had raped her to produce me, but yet 7 years later, she decided to allow him to rape her again to bring my little baby sister into the world. In a devil's advocate capacity, let's say I buy her story... wouldn't she have to be slightly demon-possessed to allow herself to take part in such evil, unholy acts and worse yet, in repetition? Of course, when I decided to put these thoughts into the air, she became defensive and assaulted me, rather than being honest and teaching me the truth. But that was the problem in and of itself.

Chapter 3 – Applying What U Learned

The breakdown in communication with my biological caused the deficits in all of my relationships until I wizened up and learned to trust my heart and research what love is really about.

Ladies when you have issues with how we as men conduct ourselves, please realize that we are that way because some woman dropped the ball when it came to educating us.

Only a woman can teach a man to be compassionate and navigate his emotions appropriately. A man never given these skills will only function as half a man, so also realize that if he is worth your time and effort, you WILL have to teach those skills to him and not assume that he will somehow magically acquire them.

I became one of these emotionally void zombies, but additionally, I developed a complex about having sex, where I always felt guilty if I ejaculated because I had been programmed to think that ejaculation was something horrific. Her fears were without warrant; they were the pent up frustrations of her life being superimposed on me through transference.

To add injury to insult I was being publicly demonized as an over-sexed teen fiend that was strung out over my stepmother, who had taken my virginity.

Where Is Love?

An event that never occurred yet had been presented widespread to every one within an ear's shot of my personal circumference of existence, as an actual and continuing event. The irony of this situation was cloaked in the fact that while she was demonizing me, she was cougarizing my baby sister's boyfriend.

I must have been a lot stronger than I remembered being because that wasn't enough to shut me down socially. Somehow I managed to meet and ultimately fall in love with my first love, M. This was certainly one of the happier times I recalled experiencing while living under the biological's roof.

Something about me being happy symbolically reminded her of how my father was off and happily indulging himself in whatever woman would have him, so of course breaking my happiness became a necessity and high priority. She began this by closely befriending my girlfriend's mother and telling her that I was some sexual predator that was going to molest her daughter. I was mortified because her mother and I were very close, as she knew how my life was at that time based on our numerous conversations.

Chapter 3 – Applying What U Learned

I had been thrown away by my biological at age 11, and all through my teen years, DYFS made continuous attempts to put me back with her, until I filed for and obtained emancipation. Often I ended up staying over their house, as a family friend, then as M's guest, and finally as the family guardian, protecting them all from M's step dad, the real child abuser and molester.

This woman that I took to as my own mother and confided all of my woes to, suddenly shifted with the wind and followed suit claiming that I had raped her daughter, further giving voice to the growing perception of me as some sex-craved deviant. Me...the young boy that always gave her money to keep their lights on? Me... the one that always knew she needed transportation and made sure that she got it? Me... the only person courageous enough to confront her despicable husband about his behavior and then attempt to protect them all from him?

Here it was the middle of summer. I found myself sitting in a courtroom, hotter than a steaming sauna. My mind was racing because I was afraid that I was going to jail, although I really had no true concept of how awful the experience really could be.

Where Is Love? 122

I was feeling rather low in spirit because I had spoken my piece and been honest about everything and yet I still was heading to jail for something I hadn't done. I scanned the courtroom and my eyes locked on the real culprit. He was smiling because he knew that I would soon be out of his way and he could go back to ravaging the children as usual. My fate now rested solidly in the hands of M.

Poor M, I didn't envy her. She had been beaten for weeks and coerced to lie on the stand and say that it was me. I had met with her some weeks earlier and I told her to do whatever they told her, to spare herself any further abuse. I guess there was something about love though, that wouldn't let her see me suffering and just let it continue. So as the judge was confirming what the offense was and her response to who had committed it against her, she broke into a spurt of revelation.

I couldn't hear anything as reality had slowed to a crawl and the pulse of the room was in sync with my every heartbeat. My throat was so dry I could barely swallow. The judge's voice was slurring into my ear... *"and Ms. M, you do realize you are under oath? Is the defendant in this room?"* *"Yes, your honor."* *"Is that the person who sexually assaulted you?"*

Chapter 3 – Applying What U Learned

"No your honor. They all keep telling me to lie on Curtis and he didn't do that your honor... he didn't rape me... Robert did!"

The courtroom exploded in yells of horror and disgust. My soul had jumped out of my body and was running around the courtroom celebrating my freedom. The bailiff was walking quickly towards Robert to secure him in their custody. He was finally gonna get his!

Unfortunately, this was the beginning of an endless stream of offenses committed under the malevolent design of the biological, which fostered the consistent procedure of stripping away my sexual security, and further tainting my scope of what engaging in sexual activity should actually look like.

First, she demonized me in place of an adult that she hated, hoping to create dissension by dividing and conquering. This was the **foundation** of her every assault. She hated my father and hated his wife even more as she was jealous of his wife's position in his life, so what better way to get at all of us than by driving the wedge between us with that horrendous lie.

Where Is Love?   124

Next, she took away my first love, but what she really did was destroy the root trust I had in her mother, who I had come to regard as my very own mother-like role model. Again, this attack centered on her very own fear of the ever-loosening grip that she had on me. Because she was losing control, she sought to destroy me instead of seeing me develop into a man of substance.

For her next contravention, she went after my first true friendship. All of these occurrences were critical events in my emotional development stage. She seemed to need to turn all of them into obstacles, rather than allowing me the normal growth process that I needed for my development. The incongruity of her actions again presented itself full-strength when she commented that I was involving myself with too many females and that I ought to socialize more with male peers.

Once more, this was at her suggestion, as had been the previous proposals turned prosecutions and here I was following through thinking that I was being obedient. I don't think I was yet capable of realizing the full scope of how despicable and miserable a person she was. I still had faith in her and believed the best in her; but there was no good to be found.

Chapter 3 – Applying What U Learned

I soon crossed paths with and befriended Cleveland J, who like myself, was the product of a dysfunctional mother that was abusive and neglectful. His older sister and her husband, who had taken him in and given him a home with them, had rescued Cleveland. I believe that our common bond was founded in the pain that we had experienced up until that point in our lives. The idea of no longer being alone in our suffering drew us so closely together that we became brothers to each other.

At first, the biological gave every sign of approving of Clevie; she always asked about him and asked me to invite him over to the house for dinner. As a matter of fact, several times I came home after school and found him there waiting in the house for me. I didn't find this to be strange or out of place at the time, but as I recall it now... it certainly does have an indecent air about it.

I began to notice that Clevie would have new sneakers and clothes all the time, but that was weird because his sister was constantly telling him that if he wanted something, he had better get a job and buy it. Whenever I brought up the new items, he became uncomfortable as though trying to avoid having to explain the basis of his funding source.

Where Is Love? 126

Finally, he came clean because I had cornered him and said if he was really supposed to be my brother, then he wouldn't hide anything from me. I think he felt that he had betrayed me long enough and so he broke down and told me that "your mother bought it for me."

I couldn't believe it.

This woman hadn't bought me any clothes since age 11 and here I was wearing the cheapest sneakers that her money could buy, while Clevie was dressing like the teen guru of 80's fashion.

His style of dress brought more females around, which was a bonus for me, so I still wasn't really that upset as I still benefitted. I honestly saw Clevie as more than just a peer; he was the older brother that I yearned for, so her actions still backfired. I wasn't mad at Clevie; I figured she was just completely unable to prioritize her own children and my only way to reach her was to do so through Clevie. So his gear increased, the girls increased, my climb up the social status ladder in school continued and the biological's frustration with our bond increased. To her, there were far too many females and this was the catalyst for her to become desperate for separating Clevie and me.

Chapter 3 – Applying What U Learned   127

The biological began lying and saying that Clevie was stealing from her and asking her to borrow money all the time. She recommended that I speak to him and supplant the idea of him not asking her for any money since she was an adult.

I guess I did so simply out of being immature and too naive to see myself being duped and misled by her misrepresentation of him. I would later be so angry with myself because I should have analyzed her complaint and realized that regardless of him asking, she did not have to grant his request. She was acting like she was the victim, but she was the mastermind, hard at work seeking the dissolution of our friendship. She additionally began to advise that he was starting to come on to me and again in my youthful immaturity, I fell prey to her consistent haranguing.

Perhaps, it was the consistent bombardment of seeing Clevie dressed well in place of me, her child that should have been receiving those goods. I thought that if I went along with her idea, she would finally rightfully accept me and address my needs. Even though I had been quite comfortable with Clevie, she kept suggesting that this act or the next was clandestine, homosexual activity.

Where Is Love? 128

I had no expertise in knowing whether that was true and I was beginning to grow quite uncomfortable with her continuous berating of my reputation. As a psyche major, I am quite sure she knew that she was subconsciously moving me towards defense against attacks on my sexuality and ultimately creating a rebellious nature towards the source of those comments... Clevie. I began to dislike being around him in any capacity because she had programmed me into believing that he was going to "try something" on me. As a family member had molested me as a youth, it wasn't hard to manipulate me into finding logic in her words.

I think back to those days and I am so ashamed because she was also indirectly implanting her hatred of homosexuals into me based on my not understanding them. This is how a greater proportion of the youth of urban America develop their disposition towards homosexuals, as African American males are often known to be homophobic. It would be a number of years before I was able to destroy that mindset and become an independent thinker in every area of my life.

The degrees of separation seemed to increase and this person whom I had once considered my brother was now my nemesis.

Chapter 3 – Applying What U Learned

The dissolution of our bond unraveled before my eyes and all the comfort of having a comrade in the navigation of life disappeared. A heart-broken Clevie moved away and I have never seen him since.

I often mourn my brother and wish for a chance to be reunited because we shared so many experiences and activities; in it all, he was always a confidant! I think that loss really awakened hostility towards the biological that could never be ameliorated. It made me thrive to get away from her and to push towards doing for myself. This was the birth of my independence! Even so, there were still some more events to navigate through prior to my absolute emancipation from the monster known as Kary.

Always, somewhere just ahead there was some maliciously constructed barrier lying just beyond the completion of the previous hurdle I had just overcome. It must have been really frustrating for her, seeing as how I always found a way to overcome each stumbling block that she put in place. She never got to see the detriment of the efforts of her hands.

Where Is Love?

The most confusing aspect of her actions was that she was the one that initialized what I did socially. She coerced me into socializing because she felt I needed a girlfriend and when M became too much of my adoration... it was a hindrance as it challenged her position, and it became an absolute trigger for her meddling once M's mother and I grew close. Then she claimed I was always to my self and I needed to learn to socialize by meeting and creating some ties with some fraternal male friends. Eventually, when I became too close to Clevie and his family, she plagued my need for his kinship by always suggesting that he was a homosexual.

As I learned to develop my own friendships, outside of her influence, she became more incensed. In addition to the physical abuse I endured, she began to seek other, more heinous methods to pollute even those experiences so that I might have no peace and solace during any waken hour of the day. The final attack I remember encountering was on my newly developed bond with Michele.

She and I had met and befriended each other independent of all assistance from outside stimulus. We had done so out of a need for each other's companionship.

Chapter 3 – Applying What U Learned   131

Michele was this gorgeous tenth-grader that every guy in school wanted to date on external observation, but they all seemed to stray away when they would engage her in conversation. It turned out that this beautiful girl possessed a very deep voice. It was something that in high school, amongst a population of immature, male adolescents, seemed the difference in why one would decide against trying to push up on her.

At that time, most males were too stupid to even consider the true character of a female as the reason for them to be attracted to one. I was always a bit different though. I was shy and awkward around her and truth be told, deep down I just assumed that I could in no way ever get with her.

It just sort of happened one day. Michele was walking to history class and she seemed to be out of her element. She wasn't smiling. She looked like she wanted to cry. No one wanted to acknowledge that they saw her in pain. I just sort of drifted into her path and asked her if I could help. Maybe it was perfect timing, maybe it was her need to have someone in her corner; whatever it was, she responded and let me in with open arms.

From that time until leaving high school, although we weren't boyfriend/girlfriend, we were inseparable.

Where Is Love?   132

No one could come between us: Our bond shone clearly for everyone to see, including the adults whom we never considered were observing us so intensely.

During our junior year in school, Michele determined that she wanted to spend time around this older guy named Buck. To me, he was evil incarnate, but females never see the danger that we males see in a male; Michele was no different in this regard.

I was hurt because here I was in love with her and assuming that we were working towards being together, meanwhile she was thinking something much different. I was her confidant and protector, but not a love interest, which was my fault seeing as how I never brought up that possibility.

So, Buck was in and he became a major thorn in my side, as I never seemed to see enough of Mikki anymore. Her infatuation seemed to center around him being older, and able to take care of her. I was constantly competing with him, indirectly, and I warned her against getting too into him. I think she thought I was jealous and I was, but I tried my best to cloak it in what was genuine concern for her safety.

I recall she had remarked about an incident that had taken place and ever since her confiding that in me, a red flag went up in my head. Buck was bad news!

Chapter 3 – Applying What U Learned   133

Since meeting him, she was skipping classes, had started smoking weed and was contemplating leaving school to move in with him... all of which had been at his suggestion.

Imagine, 20-year-old Buck was gassing up 17-year-old Michele, who was nothing more than a beautiful conquest in his sexual pursuits. I mean, I am a male; I could tell he was up to no good, but I kept hoping I would be wrong. Then a month passed and it seemed like I had no contact with Mikki at all. She hadn't been in school or anything; unbeknownst to me, she had already dropped from roll.

I walked around to her classes trying to ask questions from her teachers, who were as lost as I was. By chance, Ms. G, Michele's mom, was in school; she was really upset. She was inquiring around school about Buck. Seems Mikki had misled her into believing that he was a student in high school, which I knew wasn't true. She saw me and ran over and hugged me, which totally took me by surprise.

Ms. G was a woman that I really liked from day one because she had always embraced me based on what she saw and experienced face to face.

Where Is Love? 134

She never pre-judged me as a hoodlum, which was comforting seeing as how she was an older, white woman. The biological had polluted my brain so badly, that I automatically thought every white person would on introduction dislike me simply because I was black.

That was a fallacy of the greatest sort, but again, here I was an adolescent, wanting to believe in this woman and she was abusing her authority by lying yet once again.

I sensed that along the way of Michele and I becoming friends, her mom met the biological, who lied and told her so many ugly things about me. Ms. G began to act coldly towards me. Rightfully so, [well at least in her eyes]: as that would put any mother in a protective mode against a male that could be a detriment and distraction to their child. She began to be so different in her approach to me; she gave me the impression that I had done something that caused her to distrust me, although I hadn't. It would be a few months later, when I finally found out that she had been duped into believing that I had taken Mikki's virginity... forcefully! So, it was only logical that I was caught off guard when Ms. G walked up and hugged me. One thing that she was certain of was that I was every bit as protective of Michele as she was.

Chapter 3 – Applying What U Learned   135

She began to explain Michele's recent disappearance from school, the earlier part of which she had knowledge. She knew that I didn't like Buck, as I always had a stoned jaw at the slightest mention of his name.

Michele had gone to a party a few weeks earlier. While at the party, Buck had suggested that they take part in some illicit sexual activity with a few of his friends. Mikki being so into him, initially, didn't object. Knowing her the way I did, I assumed that she stayed quiet probably trying to determine whether he was really serious; she had a habit of waiting for things to reveal themselves before reacting. That was always her way.

As her mom told the story, her eyes filled with tears and I thought it was her disappointment with Mikki's choice, but as she went on, I began to get the entire picture. Buck continued to press the idea of sex and as the event began to unfold Michele saw that this was something inevitable; she began to object. Buck became irate, as was his manner. (Michele had previously told me how Buck tended to put his hands on her aggressively when he was upset with her.) I always assumed he was rough with her, but she always defended him and said he never had hit her.

Where Is Love? 136

I told her if he ever did, I would kill him, and she knew that I meant every word of my promise.

At the party, Buck apparently became upset and slapped her and said she was being immature about the situation. When she cried, he suggested that they all smoke some weed. Without them knowing, he put something into it. This was passed around to all of the females present and had a nullifying effect on them, so that they were easily subdued as the sexual activities began. Michele was passed amongst adult males. It was rape... plain and simple!

Buck kept Mikki at his house, the whole time working on her mentally, so that she wouldn't view it as what it actually was and tell someone... namely me. See, I was never one to shy away from being chivalrous and protective of those I cared for, so Buck had been made aware on numerous accounts that I didn't care for him. Though I was a youth, Buck was wise enough to not underestimate me as an adversary. I was a street kid for certain, but I was fairly well known for my uncanny desire to fight and defeat bigger and older opponents. He didn't want any part of me, so he was hard at work making sure that she didn't set the alarm off in my head.

Chapter 3 – Applying What U Learned   137

About a week earlier, Michele had contacted her mother and let her know that she was all right, but that she had been going through some things. I don't believe she had told her mom that all of this had happened, but she said enough for Ms. G to become alarmed. Ms. G begged Mikki to come home before something bad happened to her. As the communication between the two of them had become strained [due to her treatment of me], Mikki erupted and took her mother's concern for her well being as an attempt to control her. That was the last that Ms. G had heard from her.

So here we were in the hallway trying to find answers. We ran into a young man that Mikki had dated. I can't recall his name at the moment, but I remember him being so concerned and actually starting to cry when he turned and told me that Mikki was in the hospital. I began to cry in response to his lamenting and lost my cool and punched/shattered the glass in the hallway trophy case. Had I gone searching the hospitals on my own, I doubt I would have found Mikki, because I would have never checked the hospital where I found her.

Call it coincidence, I'll call it providence, but I just so happened to have to be taken to the hospital to stitch my hand up.

Where Is Love? 138

Who do you think I saw lying on a stretcher in the emergency room?

Was that a bruise on her cheek? Why was she screaming so incessantly? Was that Chuck with her? He looked like he was trying to hush her.... Was he grabbing her? I ran over to Mikki and asked her, "what was the matter?" She continued screaming.

Her doctor came out and he asked whether I knew Mikki. I told him I did. He requested that I come into the exam area where she was stationed. He then asked how close we were, to which I responded, "like brother and sister." He suddenly displayed a look of relief.

He began to recount the events that had caused Mikki to come to the hospital; apparently, she had been at a party and someone [Buck] had given her LSD and she was currently experiencing the effects of the drug. She had been found wandering around outside in the cold and screaming loudly. I began to tear and cry as he told me the account. I couldn't believe Buck had done such a low thing. How could he possibly claim to love Mikki and then cause her to experience something so horrendous?

Chapter 3 – Applying What U Learned

According to my understanding, she would not be free of the effects of this drug for several years to come (or maybe for the rest of her life), as it was believed that people tended to relapse and trip again in the future even from a "one and only" usage of this drug. The possibility of my dear Michele again reliving the horror of this night and me possibly being nowhere around to protect her sickened me. I already felt guilty for what had happened because I believed I had deserted her out of my jealousy of her being with Buck. I learned the most concrete definition of loyalty that day.

I somehow sensed that she would never be the same again after this event and I determined to never allow anyone close to me to suffer without me attempting to eradicate any potential harm to them ever again. Michele and I remained close for the first few months after that took place, but eventually we parted ways. I think that she always felt embarrassed by what had happened and she ran away from me to avoid feeling judged, although I never blamed her... I loved her!

Michele actually represented for me the beginning of my chivalrous nature and my need to rescue those in my circle from all hurt and harm.

Where Is Love? 140

I believe this also spilled over into my sexual nature and caused me to desire to be absolutely perfect as a sexual partner.

I find it impossible to engage in making love to a woman and not be able to make her orgasm; especially, since I know the dire state of most women's sexual experience. I carry a sort of shame for how the men objectify women or fall short of treating women as ladies. A significant portion of women complains openly that they have never been pleased and I determined to never be selfish in the pursuit of my own sexual pleasure.

I began my sexual history nobly, at least I thought so, but it transformed into a denial of allowing myself any pleasure at all. At the impetus of all of these different occurrences, I was consistently being accosted by haunting remembrances of the biological's variation of Christian justification for every deed that she illicitly approved and disapproved of. At the same time I was harangued by the implicit lies that were used to "scare" me into doing what she considered "right."

Listen to me, ***nothing done between a woman*** and man should be viewed as nasty, if both parties have come together in agreement that those deeds are for their mutual enjoyment.

Chapter 3 – Applying What U Learned

If one partner expects certain acts to take place, they have to be open to reciprocity. Furthermore, they both have to practice the concept of preserving their privacy. Best friends, brothers, sisters, associates, whoever... should not be privy to the knowledge of what takes place between you and your partner behind closed doors. Outside opinions tend to poison the natural mindset of a couple and this can eventually cause either partner to alter their own way of interacting in the relationship.

Yes, I experienced this myself and it yielded the best point of reference ever. The event gave birth to my mantra a man will never learn without loss. This sting of emotional pain creates the best foundation for permanently improving the thinking pattern and behavior of a man.

If you haven't gotten it yet... let me be clear [the techniques]...

The purpose of this final section is to clearly provide practical examples of how to accept each other's problematic areas and improve on your ability to embrace and understand your mate. You have been provided with a range of my thoughts and theories on love between two adults.

Where Is Love? 142

No matter how intensely I attempted to present my words clearly, I just believe that giving examples best helps to bring home a summary of what I have intended to share with you. By far, these are not all the possible scenarios that can be encountered, but hopefully these are typical of a large majority of the readers' relationships. I have tried to present unisex examples, so that either sex might apply the scenarios to their particular relationships. Allowing everyone an opportunity to put into practice what they have read, should help to consolidate the material that was covered and bring home the message of the entire book. In this manner, I may ultimately have achieved my purpose for having authored this work; to see people in a relationship learn to love each other in a way that pleases each of them.

1] Your partner is already conditioned to be fearful of speaking intimately; break that fear by building their security. This is achieved by you acting out the opposite polarity of emotional investment. Let's say your partner tends to always shy away from having deep conversations on the phone. This time you slightly initiate the conversation. *This guarantees that the conversation is on target.*

Chapter 3 – Applying What U Learned

Then you begin to show shyness towards actually talking about the juiciest tidbits of info. This will appeal to your partner, because the topic is irresistible and their mind has been captivated and they want to participate. Usually their fear stifles their ability to do so, but today they see you struggling to take part and this enables them to speak. They see the stronger partner working through a state of vulnerability. *It gives them confidence to speak openly, when they see that they can initiate a strong conversation and for once be the leader in an intimate conversation. Building their security breaks your partner's fear. The stronger communicator acting in an opposite role of their usual self achieves this.*

2] You feel as though you are too often taken for granted and it drives you crazy knowing that your mate doesn't value you as you feel they should. You need to address this head on, because if you allow the situation to drag on, your pain will continue. You must be sure to **remind** your mate of **your** value and the fact that you are **aware** of your value.

Men all too often don't realize the value of their mate and don't learn it until they lose them.

Where Is Love?

Women realize their value, and feel owed the attention, since they have endured the lack thereof far too long, yet remain silent. *Being appreciated for your value provides validation that you are a priority.* No one wants to be taken for granted. Make sure you show that you appreciate your mate, as that is the best example of how they should treat you. *Leading by example provides you with an opportunity to set the standard in your relationship of being willing to take risks for the betterment of the union.*

3] Dealing with the very cocky attitude of a partner that believes that they are gifted sexually, when in fact, that partner happens to be awful.

To address this properly, you must refer back to the basis of your foundation, communication. This partner needs an ample dosage of honesty, laced with tact spoken mercifully. *Not addressing this person head on, is the same as simply agreeing to their commentary and even worse, condemning you to having to accept their abject efforts as their best foot forward so to speak.* Make direct eye contact and ask your partner if they are open to a discussion. Inform them that things will be stated that may be unpleasant.

Chapter 3 – Applying What U Learned

Remind your partner that if you are truly a couple, then it's in both your interests to be open & accepting of criticism and able to listen to each other. Confirm their willingness by asking them, "do you understand and are you willing to listen to everything I am going to say quietly until I am finished? Now remember that I love you and this isn't a personal attack on you, but rather a dialogue between us to improve our situation." *This lays the ground rules for the conversation and assures the partner that a certain level of comfort can be taken, since these things aren't being said to attack or hurt them. Because they have agreed to participate, they should have better reactions to the discussion.*

4] To improve communication between you and your partner play my word game. In far too many relationships, the belief in "women being from Venus and men from Mars" philosophy seems to present itself. Unfortunately, partners usually just accept this void in their dialogue as something that must continually be impervious to improvement because somehow that's just how it is biologically. Nothing could be farther from the truth. The real problem lies in each partner not being able to interpret the meaning of the words used in the conversation.

Where Is Love? 146

They can both be using the exact same words, in a similar order, but the meaning can be so different it's alarming. To assist couples in being able to decipher what each means, I have devised a little game that I like to have couples play.

Each partner gets a sheet of paper and something to write with. One elects to go first and writes down a list of words commonly exchanged between them. The other partner copies down that exact same list. They begin by going down their list and writing what each word means until they have completed the list. Once they are done, they exchange their sheets and go over the definitions. To their amazement, most couples are blown away by the results. *The very same words often solicit a different meaning for each partner. This is critical in learning to understand and accept the unique thoughts of each partner.* No, he or she hasn't been trying to cause you strife by their responses during your talks. They simply don't interpret the subjects under discussion the same, but *by compiling lists of the couple's common language and gaining the ability to anticipate how each interprets the content, each can learn to frame their statements in a way that allows each a fair chance at answering the questions without the ambiguity of misinterpretation.*

Chapter 3 – Applying What U Learned

The endless cycle of anger that usually accompanies an expansive chat can now be usurped; the truer intent can be discerned.

5] Men feel as though a woman should naturally know how to be submissive to them. This is not easily a state that the relationship will exist in, unless the man is able to understand the importance of respecting and yielding to a higher calling in his and by extension, their lives.

It should never be his expectation that she can drop everything and follow him. until he has led by example and showed her that he can drop his pride and follow a higher conscious. In doing this, he gives her assurance that he believes in something bigger than himself and that his judgment is not simply based on folly or his fleeting emotions. He shows absolute courage and the ability to be faithful and loyal. He erases her fear of risking her heart for the betterment of the couple because he has shown restraint, submission to deeds of the spirit and control over his flesh.

6] As partners in a relationship, each must come to appreciate that the other is still an individual.

Where Is Love?   148

Because they are together, that does not mean that one should exert force over the other or try to dominate the actions, thoughts, and intentions of the other.

In love, there should be an ability to accept the whole person, especially the side that each considers as the flawed aspect of the other. To simply believe that each should be in some state of absolute perfection is not even a smart perception of the truth. A stronger foundation is formed when each is able to love the other *in spite* of what each *dislikes* about the other.

It's always easy to attach ourselves to anything that we like, but can we show equal enthusiasm towards that person when we are not on the best of terms. This is of course no easy task, as a greater amount of human beings tend to lack the patience to even attempt this. So in order to develop this skill, one should address their mate in a state of remembrance when something unpleasant is to be embraced. You take yourself to a thought of when you did something that was hurtful to another and they found the strength to forgive you. *The somberness of that experience should set your mind in the correct state for accepting a deficit in your partner because you are actively reminding yourself of your own faults.*

Chapter 3 – Applying What U Learned

This should be done every time you need to accept your partner's shortcomings until you are able to generate compassion beyond your anger on your own.

This not only will draw your partner closer to you, but they may actually seek to improve on that deficit in appreciation of your being willing to accept them in spite of it.

7] Learn to hold each other down regardless of arguments and temporary ill will; there should be no cheating because of some punk ass chat going wrong. That's looking for an excuse. *This is your other half.* To my brothers out there, *this woman was created to be a comfort for you against all woes of the world. She is your rib. A woman's heart should be so lost in righteousness that a man needs to rejuvenate his spirit and kinship with nature in order to find her.* If that is the journey that most of us are willing to travel to find the love of our lives, then what sense should it make to blow everything in an instant by reacting with as much civility as a hungry bear. *We have a duty to act in a noble manner. That's why we have been charged with providing for her and protecting her. It was never meant for her to step up and take the lead.*

Where Is Love?

That was our ancient rite, which we cowardly set aside to indulge in the practices of a mindset that is all too foreign to our souls.

8] Keep communication as the centerpiece of your relationship. Talk, talk some more, and then continue to talk. Chances are if you can't talk too long, then you can't listen to each other either. If that's so, then there is no need to even waste each other's time.

Just that quickly you will have shown that you cannot appreciate your partner for the long haul; your like for each other was only a shroud cloaking momentary lust.

Communication is something that a couple can't fake because it shows an unselfish, true interest in the well being of one's partner. When one doesn't recognize the worth of their partner, there is no true foundation for growth and mutual respect was never established. Communication serves as proof that the person you have chosen to be with is someone that you respect, but more importantly, is someone that you like. Communication is the result of investing serious time in engaging in learning someone and creating a foundation of trust with them.

Chapter 3 – Applying What U Learned

It's not a simple thing; when you find partners of a couple complaining that it's a major task to talk to the person that they claim to love more than anyone else in this world, they have a serious dilemma. Far too often, I have observed people simulating something closer to torment when they have to take time and embrace in sharing a dialogue with their partner. I watch the behavior, listen to the complaints and just shake my head in disbelief.

9] Let each partner be who they are... don't punish a good person for the errors of that past ass who actually caused the scars on your heart. It's far too unfair of a burden to toss on the back of a new person that is enamored of you and only wanting to love you until the end. No matter how hard the new person loves you, until you are ready to let go of the pass, they can never fill that void in you. They will only end up sustaining blows never deserved by them. *It's a very selfish thing to solicit the heart of someone who is pure and untainted as far as your heart's battles and cast them in the role of existing simply to heal a scar that they have no knowledge of or worse yet, the recipient of your abuse because you have transferred the hurt of the past onto them.*

10] Make time for each other. Always remember what it was that first brought you into each other's universe and make a show of appreciating that uniqueness.

Far too often, I meet couples and they complain of the relationship no longer having that fire it used to have. The wife is critical of the husband eyeing and desiring younger girls, but within that complaint, is the sole solution to the problem. He desires the freedom that a younger mind naturally exudes. Has his wife become a creature of habit that has forgotten what it was like to have fun?

Recently, in an interview on the Monique show, Tamala Mann famed singer and actress of the Tyler Perry plays, stated and I quote, "I refuse to let anyone out do me when it comes to my man!" That is something serious to consider when they have been married for over 20 years. But, she achieves success by keeping herself up. Her hair is done, her clothes are clean, fit well and are stylish, and she carries herself in a positive manner. All of this is extremely attractive to any man. Men, we should adhere to the same principles and add to that the need to maintain good health and a shapely physique. It's critical to be each other's eye candy, as it helps to assist the partner in maintaining eyes for only you.

Chapter 3 – Applying What U Learned

11] Read, learn, understand and consistently practice 1 Corinthians 13:4-8... say no more! This verse is the only set of data that I know that accurately reflects exactly the entire concept of love.

One might consider all of the listed attributes as difficult to practice, but if that is the case, then you will know suddenly, that the person isn't for you, since there shouldn't be such a thing as a difficulty in loving someone. Your partner is supposed to be just that: the complementary half of you that is responsible for making the creation and maintenance of your happiness their privilege and priority.

FINAL THOUGHTS

Let me just say that scribing this assimilation of my
thoughts on love and the causes that bring it out of
alignment along with regaining the ability to bring it
back into focus appropriately, has allowed me to travel
on a ride through my very own experiences, pains, joys,
failures, triumphs, to further assist me in growing into a
great man... the man I always longed to know.

The friend I always wanted.

The lover that I never had.

The man that I am now.

A king.

Only a righteous-hearted man can make himself a king
and now that I have become one,
it has become ever more relevant to pass on the
knowledge of becoming a king
and then teaching young men how to
Stay a King.

Likewise, there are the princesses
and it is our job to edify and cherish them
and set them high as our queens.

Then ladies,
you are expected to maintain your nobility and foster
the positive effect of being one with your partner.

Final Thoughts

* * *

You all have been such great patrons of this first work and I hope that you will continue to grow with me, as I continue to become an even more intense writer providing a needed commentary for society.
Until we meet between the pages of my next endeavor, may my love, commitment and need to fulfill my obligation to uplift and build our humanity, set off the very same obligation in each and every one of you.
From my Spirit, to your ear,
Prose

Where is love... its in you!

Write in Black Inc.®

Where Is Love?　　　　　　　　　　　　156

I know that there is one person that I need to share the success of this book with that I chose to withhold from the book. Her name is Ruth Skerrett. This woman came into my life and not simply befriended me, but became my everything. My confidant, my nurturer, my shoulder, my rock... she allowed me to catch a glimpse of what I would search for in a woman for the rest of my life.

Ruth, if you by chance get your hands on this book, know that I didn't desert you at all. I was forced to leave earlier than I had intended; to go fight in Desert Storm. We were supposed to hang all that weekend and I was going to break it to you and confess how deeply in love I was with you. The president decided to send us in early and I got snatched up right after leaving you, so this revelation never made its way to your ears.

I have spent the last 20 plus years seeking you and have been heartbroken over the loss of you for over half my life. I wish I could have said all the things that I hid away and I didn't mean to cheat you out of knowing... I was just scared of the potential loss.

You were my everything!

My personal search

I was shy and a coward, so it just seemed safer to accept where we were, rather than to push further and end up losing you forever. You knew all of my pain and the suffering I had sustained as a child and you still stayed around and made me feel worthwhile. When my flesh and blood abandoned me, you were there.

Ironically, I still loss you and it has plagued me for years.

You more than every other woman that I have mentioned, laid the base of the foundation of the man I have become and I thank you for every kind and tender word, for always moving to protect my heart, and for loving me just as I was even when I couldn't love myself. Wherever you are in this world, you are treasured and cherished in this life and beyond.

Forever, I love you with all my heart Ruth.

Where Is Love?   158

Grandma Dot Taylor & Aunt Teesha

I have always wanted the opportunity to take my time
and in some flambouyant way put on display, my
appreciation and love for the two of you saving my life.
You both wanted me, when even my own parents had no
place in their hearts for me. To selflessly take not just
from your heart, but your pocket to show me how much
you love me means more than I can even convey in
words. It earned you both my lifetime loyalty.

Teesha the struggles you endured personally may have
been many, but you raised several fine children. We are
blessed that you loved us... never forget that. You can't
minimize your parenting success simply because of
some skeletons in the closet... we loved and do love you
always. We NEVER saw you as a failure or
embarassment. We were HONORED to have you
looking after us.
Grandma... I ran away because I was so hurt that I had
disappointed you.
Running the streets, the hustling, fighting... all of those
acts were committed by a little boy that just could not
understand why his own mama never wanted him.
I hope I've finally done you proud!

Uncle Julius & Aunt Betty

You know I couldn't finish this book without mentioning
the impact you both had on me.
Unc you are the model of manhood that I have always
modeled myself after.
It takes a phenomenal man to be able to move to heal
the scars of a child. I wasn't your child, but from the
first time I walked into your home, you and Aunt Betty
made it my business to know that I was yours.
It made the difference to a child that thought that he
had no worth in anyone's eyes.
You were so concerned for my well being when my own
and father and mother could care less.
Aunt Betty... you are as close to my idea of a saint as I
have come to witness in this life!
I got my spirituality from you.
Observing you grow into a strong woman of God and
putting the righteous principals to use day to day,
I was humbled and wanted to follow your example.
The two of you are my parents in my eyes and it shall
remain so forever.
I just thank you both so much for loving me!

About the Author

I initially picked up a **P**en in my attempt to vindicate myself from a lifetime of abuse and neglect.
I figured it would be the best way to get back at all those that hurt me; that was a younge**R**, immature me. Somewhere along the way, I began to learn of what it meant t**O** be a king and Stay a King.
Although I wasn't one yet, I desired to become the best model of me that had ever exi**S**ted.
I opened up and began to share thoughts on topics that we, as members of soci**E**ty, all tend to suppress.

The need had been recognized and my fervor for being a hero took hold of me in its infancy.

May your minds accept my thoughts expressed through my pen.

Author Contact Information

Prose the Writer

www.facebook.com/WriteInBlackInc

writeinblackink@gmail.com

www.iwriteinblackinc.com

862-200-PENS (7367)

writeinblackink.blogspot.com

CPSIA information can be obtained at www.ICGtesting.com
Printed in the USA
BVOW011208240313

316255BV00005B/53/P